Phishing Detection Using Content-Based Image Classification

T0353601

Phishing Detection Using Content-Based Image Classification

Shekhar Khandelwal and Rik Das

CRC Press
Taylor & Francis Group
Boca Raton London New York

CRC Press is an imprint of the
Taylor & Francis Group, an **informa** business
A CHAPMAN & HALL BOOK

First edition published 2022
by CRC Press
6000 Broken Sound Parkway NW, Suite 300, Boca Raton, FL 33487-2742

and by CRC Press
4 Park Square, Milton Park, Abingdon, Oxon, OX14 4RN

CRC Press is an imprint of Taylor & Francis Group, LLC

© 2022 Shekhar Khandelwal and Rik Das

ISBN: 9781032108537 (hbk)
ISBN: 9781032265025 (pbk)
ISBN: 9781003217381 (ebk)

DOI: 10.1201/9781003217381

Typeset in Times
by Deanta Global Publishing Services, Chennai, India

Contents

Preface

Phishing is one of the most prominent cybercrimes which has posed significant threat to transactions over the world wide web. Visual similarity of a forged website to its genuine counterpart often misleads web users to fall prey to this malicious activity. Hence, it has become imperative to build awareness about the basics of phishing within cybersecurity domains and to identify the different techniques used by phishers to attack web users. It is evident that the various anti-phishing initiatives have instigated a race between phishers and anti-phishers, leading to constant innovation by both parties to stay ahead in the game.

The popularity of machine learning and deep learning techniques has leveraged the research using image processing-based phishing detection techniques. Researchers have faced various challenges in detecting phishing using website images. A tabular comparison and summary of various related works is discussed in this volume to provide a clear historical perspective for phishing detection. Open-source programming languages like Python have implemented several Convolutional Neural Network (CNN)-based phishing detection statistical models. A step-by-step guide to building a CNN Model is discussed to make the reader familiar with assorted approaches to preventing phishing. Creation of the transfer learning-based CNN model using various off-the-shelf CNN architectures has proved to be useful in deep learning-based phishing detection. Robust feature extraction from website images using representation learning is also explored to design useful descriptors for identifying duplicate websites. The ground-up approach of extracting image representations is implemented using various off-the-shelf CNN architectures like VGGNet, ResNet, DenseNet, and so on. Machine learning models are created using pre-processed image features and performance comparison between various models.

Finally, feature dimension reduction and fusion-based techniques are explored for creating strong feature vectors to implement content-based image classification-based phishing detection. The diversified approaches discussed in this book provide the reader with a 360° overview and a stepping stone to experience this interdisciplinary domain of phishing detection using image content of the websites.

This book is intended for graduates and undergraduates from assorted backgrounds such as data science, network security and research, software developers and as a reference book for scientists, researchers, lecturers, and tutors, as well as for academic and corporate libraries.

Shekhar Khandelwal

Rik Das

Authors

Shekhar Khandelwal is a Data Scientist and works with Ernst & Young (EY), Bangalore, India for the Data & Analytics team. He has extensive experience of around 15 years in the industry, and has worked across every sphere of the software development life cycle. He has worked as a product developer, industry solutions developer, data engineer, data scientist and Cloud developer. Previously, he worked for IBM Software Labs, where he also got a chance to work for industrial IoT-based IBM cognitive product development and client deployment using various Watson tools and technologies. He is an industry leader solving challenging computer vision, NLP and predictive analytics-based problems using machine learning and deep learning.

Dr. Rik Das is currently a Lead Software Engineer in Computer Vision Research at Siemens Advanta, India. Previously he was with Xavier Institute of Social Service, Ranchi, as an Assistant Professor for the Post Graduate Program in Information Technology.

Dr. Das has over 17 years of experience in industrial and academic research. He was professionally associated with many leading universities and institutes in India, including Narsee Monjee Institute of Management Studies (NMIMS) (deemed-to-be-university), Globsyn Business School and Maulana Abul Kalam Azad University of Technology.

Dr. Das has a Ph.D. (Tech.) in Information Technology from the University of Calcutta. He has also received his M.Tech. (Information Technology) from the University of Calcutta after his B.E. (Information Technology) from the University of Burdwan, West Bengal, India.

Dr. Das has over 18 years of professional experience in the IT industry and traditional academia and with EduTech companies and has carried out collaborative research with various leading universities and institutes in India and abroad. He has an early career stint in Business Development and Project Marketing with Great Eastern Impex Pvt. Ltd., Zenith Computers Ltd. and so on.

Dr. Rik Das is appointed as a "Distinguished Speaker" by the Association of Computing Machinery (ACM), New York, for a tenure of three years initiating from July2020. He was featured in uLektz Wall of Fame as one of the "Top 50 Tech Savvy Academicians in Higher Education across India" for the year 2019. He is also a Member of the International Advisory Committee of AI-Forum, UK.

Dr. Das is awarded "Professional Membership" of the "Association of Computing Machinery (ACM)", New York, for the year 2020–2021. He is the recipient of the prestigious "InSc Research Excellence Award" hosted in the year 2020. Dr. Das is conferred with the Best Researcher Award at International Scientist Awards on Engineering, Science and Medicine for the year 2021. He is also the recipient of the Best Innovation Award in the Computer Science category at UILA Awards 2021.

Dr. Das has carried out collaborative research with professionals from companies like Philips-Canada, Cognizant Technology Solutions and TCS. His keen interest in the application of machine learning and deep learning techniques for designing computer-aided diagnosis systems has resulted in joint publications of research articles with professors and researchers from various universities abroad, including the College of Medicine, University of Saskatchewan, Canada; Faculty of Electrical Engineering and Computer Science, VSB Technical University of Ostrava, Ostrava, Czech Republic; and Cairo University, Giza, Egypt. He has filed and published two Indian patents consecutively during the year 2018 and 2019 and has over 40 international publications to date with reputed publishers like IEEE, Springer, Emerald and Inderscience. He has also authored three books in the domain of content-based image classification and has edited three volumes to date with IGI Global, CRC Press and De Gruyter, Germany. He has chaired several sessions in International Conferences on Artificial Intelligence and Machine Learning as a domain expert.

Dr. Rik Das has served as an invited speaker in various national and international technical events, conclaves, meetups and refresher courses on data analytics, artificial intelligence, machine learning, deep learning, image processing and e-learning organized and hosted by prominent bodies like the University Grants Commission (Human Resource Development Centre), the Confederation of Indian Industry (CII), Software Consulting Organizations, MHRD initiative under Pandit Madan Mohan Malviya National Mission on Teachers and Teaching, IEEE Student Chapters and Computer Science/ Information Technology Departments of leading universities.

Dr. Rik Das has a YouTube channel "Curious Neuron" to disseminate free knowledge and information to larger communities in the domain of machine learning, research and development and open source programming languages. He is always open to discussing new research and project ideas for collaborative work and techno-managerial consultancies.

Phishing and Cybersecurity

1

Phishing is a cybercrime intended to trap innocent web users into a counterfeit website, which is visually similar to its legitimate counterpart. Initially, users are redirected to phishing websites through various social and technical routing techniques. Unaware of the illegitimacy of the website, the users may then provide their personal information such as user id, password, credit card details or bank account details, to name a few. The phishers use such information to steal money from banks, damage a brand's image or even commit graver crimes like identity theft. Although many phishing detection and prevention techniques are available in the existing literature, the advent of smart machine learning and deep learning methods has widened their scope in the cyber-security world.

STRUCTURE

In this chapter, we will cover the following topics:

- Basics of phishing in cybersecurity
- Phishing detection techniques
  - List (whitelist/blacklist)-based
  - Heuristics (predefined rules)-based
  - Visual similarity-based
- Race between phishers and anti-phishers
- Computer vision-based phishing detection approach

DOI: 10.1201/9781003217381-1

OBJECTIVE

After studying this chapter, you should know what phishing is and how it affects everyone who has a web footprint. You will learn about the various ways phishers attack web users and how users can protect themselves from phishing attacks. You will also know the various phishing detection mechanisms that play a vital role in protecting web users from phishing attacks.

BASICS OF PHISHING IN CYBERSECURITY

Phishing is a term derived from fishing, by replacing "f" with "ph", but contextually they mean the same (*Phishing Definition & Meaning | What Is Phishing?*, n.d.). Just as fish get trapped in fishing nets, so too are innocent web users being trapped by phishing websites. Phishing websites are counterfeit websites that are visually similar to their legitimate counterparts. Web users are redirected to phishing websites by various means. Figure 1.1 depicts the various techniques employed by phishers to circulate spam messages that contain links to phishing websites.

Jain and Gupta (2017) stated that spreading infected links is the starting point of any phishing attack. Once users have received the infected links in their inbox through any of the phishing attack mechanisms shown in Figure 1.1, whether they click on those links or not depends on the users' awareness. Hence, at the outset, user awareness is the most important, yet most ignored, anti-phishing mechanism.

But to protect users from phishing attacks, anti-phishers have explored many technical anti-phishing mechanisms by considering even novice and technically inept users.

PHISHING DETECTION TECHNIQUES

Phishing detection mechanisms are broadly categorized into four groups, as depicted in Figure 1.2 (Khonji et al., 2013):

1) List (whitelist/blacklist)-based
2) Heuristics (pre-defined rules)-based
3) Visual similarity-based
4) AI/ML-based

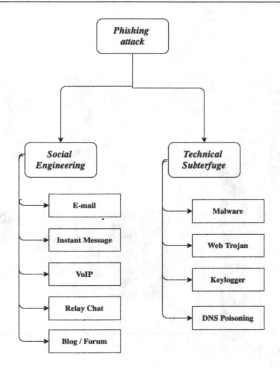

FIGURE 1.1 Types of phishing attacks.

List (Whitelist/Blacklist)-Based

In a list-based anti-phishing mechanism, a whitelist and blacklist of URLs are created and are compared against a suspicious website URL to conclude whether the website under scrutiny is a phishing website or a legitimate one (Jain & Gupta, 2016) (Prakash et al., 2010).

There are various limitations with the list-based approach, namely:

1) It is dependent on a third-party service provider that captures and maintains such lists, like Google safe browsing API (*Google Safe Browsing|Google Developers*, n.d.).
2) Adding a newly deployed phishing website to the white/blacklist is a process that takes time. First such a website has to be identified, and then it has to be listed. Since the average lifetime of a phishing website is 24–32 hours, hence zero-day phishing attacks, this is a serious limitation (*Zero-Day (Computing) – Wikipedia*, n.d.).

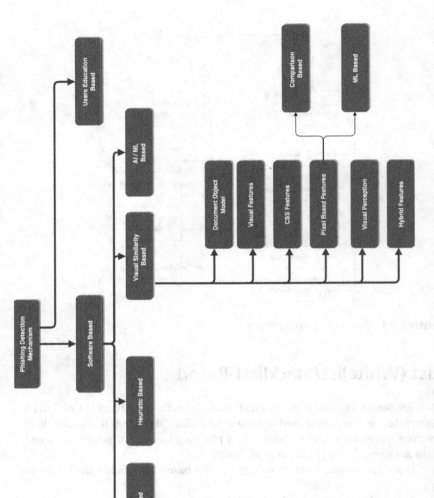

FIGURE 1.2 Phishing detection mechanisms.

Heuristics (Pre-Defined Rules)-Based

In heuristic-based approaches, various website features like image, text, URL and DNS records are extracted and used to build a rule-based engine or a machine learning-based classifier to classify a given website as phishing or legitimate. Although heuristic-based approaches are among quite effective anti-phishing mechanisms, some of their drawbacks have been pointed out by Varshney et al. (2016):

1) The time and computational resources required for training are too high.
2) Heuristic-based applications cannot be used as a browser plugin.
3) The approach would be ineffective once scammers discovered the key features that can be used to bypass the rules.

Visual Similarity-Based

Visual similarity-based techniques are very useful in detecting phishing since phishing websites look similar to their legitimate counterparts. These techniques use visual features like text content, text format, DOM (Document Object Model) features, CSS features, website images, etc., to detect phishing. Here, DOM-, CSS-, HTML tags- and pixel-based features are compared to their legitimate counterparts in order to make a decision.

Within pixel-based techniques, there are two broad categories through which phishing detection is achieved. One approach is through comparison of visual signatures of suspicious website images with the stored visual signatures of legitimate websites. For example, hand-crafted image features like SIFT (Scale Invariant Feature Transform) (Lowe, 2004), SURF (Speeded Up Robust Features) (Bay et al., 2006), HOG (Histogram of Oriented Gradient) (Li et al., 2016), LBP (Local Binary Patterns) (Nhat & Hoang, 2019), DAISY (Tola et al., 2010) and MPEG7 (Rayar, 2017) are extracted from the legitimate websites and stored in a local datastore, which is used as a baseline for comparing similar features from the websites under scrutiny. And based on the comparison result, the phishing website is classified. Another approach is machine learning- or deep learning classifier-based, where image features of phishing and legitimate webpages are extracted and used to build a classifier for phishing detection.

RACE BETWEEN PHISHERS AND ANTI-PHISHERS

Phishers are continually upgrading their skills and devising new and innovative ways to bypass all the security layers and deceive innocent users. For example, many heuristic-based approaches validate if the website under suspicion is SSL-enabled or not, to determine whether it is a legitimate website or a phishing website. However, nowadays, the number of phishing websites hosted on HTTPS is also increasing significantly.

Similarly, for other significant predictors of a phishing website, phishers may find ways to bypass all the rules employed to detect phishing, which is evident from the upward trend of phishing attacks attempted in recent years. Hence, if phishers find a way to bypass list-based, heuristic-based and hybrid anti-phishing detection mechanisms, to redirect the users to the phishing website, then the image processing-based anti-phishing techniques play a vital role in providing the final security layer to the web users. In this book, we propose numerous machine learning and deep learning methods that manually extract features using computer vision techniques for phishing detection. However, there are two major limitations of these methods. First, these methods utilize a comparison-based technique that requires creating a large datastore of baseline values of legitimate websites. Second, these methods rely on manual hand-crafted feature extraction techniques.

Image Processing-Based Phishing Detection Techniques

2

Studies and statistics suggest that phishing is still a pressing issue in the world of cybercrime. Despite all the research, innovations and developments made in phishing detection mechanisms, revenue losses through phishing attacks are humongous, and therefore there is a pressing need to continue research on various aspects of phishing, as anti-phishers are in an arms race with phishers. And in order to win this race, anti-phishers need to think outside the box and close all the doors before phishers enter users' premises for theft.

Assume that phishers are able to make users bypass all the list-based, heuristic-based and user awareness-based approaches, and finally made the user to land on the phishing website. At this stage, by analyzing the website image, using image processing techniques to classify whether the website in question is legitimate or phishing, can be considered as a final resort to warn users for phishing attack.

Additionally, list-based approaches cannot protect users from zero-day attacks, and heuristics-based approaches are only good until phishers decipher the underlying rules, because once they discover the underlying rules, they find a way to bypass them. Hence, image processing techniques can provide a last resort for the user's protection.

DOI: 10.1201/9781003217381-2

STRUCTURE

In this chapter, we will cover the following topics:

- Image processing-based phishing detection techniques
  - Comparison-based techniques
  - Machine learning-based techniques
- Challenges in phishing detection using website images
- Comparison of techniques
- Summary of phishing detection using image processing techniques

OBJECTIVE

After studying this chapter, you will know various anti-phishing techniques previously invented and deployed using image processing approaches for detecting phishing. You will also understand the related technological challenges and limitations. Additionally, you will be provided with a detailed comparison of all the techniques previously implemented for detecting phishing.

IMAGE PROCESSING-BASED PHISHING DETECTION TECHNIQUES

Image processing-based phishing detection has offered two different solutions. These solutions can be categorized as comparison-based or machine learning-based. In both categories, the feature vector for certain image descriptors from the image of a suspicious website is extracted. Now, for comparison-based solutions, the difference in the visual appearance of the website in question is compared with their legitimate counterpart and is calculated. Based on a certain threshold for their visual difference, it is concluded whether the website in question is phishing or not.

In the first category of solutions, the visual signatures of a legitimate website are stored in a local database, and the visual signatures of the suspicious website are extracted in runtime. Then the visual signatures of the suspicious website are compared with those available in the datastore. Based on the similarity score, the suspicious website is classified as legitimate or fake.

Comparison-Based Techniques

Rosiello et al. (2007) proposed a layout similarity-based approach using the DOM of the web page for detecting phishing called DOMAntiPhish. In this approach, the details of the DOM in the form of a vector are stored in the cache of the system, and when a user enters the same credentials in another website, again the DOM vectors are extracted from the new website and are compared with those stored in the system cache. If the information matches a certain threshold value, then the domain is compared, and if the domain matches, it's considered a legitimate website. But if the domain doesn't match, then it's considered a phishing website, which must have copied the DOM content of the legitimate website and deployed it on a different domain. Such techniques have their own limitations in terms of their effectiveness and scaling capabilities, as they only compare the DOM details already stored on the system. But the takeaway from this approach is comparison of the domain of the suspicious website once the phishing alarm is raised; in this case, suspicion is raised through DOM comparison.

Similarly, various solutions utilize other visual features of the suspicious website to extract and compare with the already-stored legitimate website profile to detect phishing.

PhishZoo (Afroz & Greenstadt, 2011) is one such solution that uses URL, text contents, SSL (Secure Socket Layer) certificates, images (especially logo) on the web page, HTML contents and scripts. In this approach, a local datastore is maintained, which stores the URL, SSL, images, HTML contents and scripts metadata of the legitimate websites. During runtime, similar details are extracted from the website to which the user navigates, and if matching URL and SSL are found in the local datastore, then the website is declared legitimate. If they don't match, then other details like image and HTML contents are matched. If a match is not found, then the website is declared legitimate, otherwise it is declared as phishing, since all other contents match but not the URL and the SSL.

One of the noticeable heuristic-based anti-phishing mechanisms that also uses images of a web page is GoldPhish (Dunlop et al., 2010), which uses OCR technology (*Optical Character Recognition Wikipedia*, n.d.) to extract text from the logo of a web page. Once the brand name is extracted, GoldPhish uses Google's PageRank algorithm to get the top five web pages using the extracted text from the logo. Then the suspicious web page domain is compared with the top five domains returned from the Google search API, and if the suspicious website domain does not match with any of the five domains, then it's declared a phishing website.

GoldPhish is different from other comparison-based image processing mechanisms since it stores no data in any local datastore; it instead uses Google APIs to extract information at runtime. But the downside of this approach is that it is dependent on OCR technology service providers and is also dependent on Google's PageRank algorithm.

GoldPhish utilizes OCR technology to extract the logo of the web page, while Verilogo (Wang, 2010) uses a SIFT image descriptor (Lowe, 2004) to extract the logo of the given suspicious website.

Verilogo not only extracts the logo using a SIFT descriptor, but also deploys multi-level phishing detection mechanisms. If the logo of the extracted website does not match any logo in the local datastore, the website is assumed legitimate, since there is no data available for comparison, and hence the user is allowed to continue on the website. Therefore the phishing detection capability of Verilogo is limited only to the brands whose legitimate logos are stored in the datastore.

Furthermore, if the logo matches with the existing logo in the datastore, two more levels of detection are employed: first the DNS lookup of the website, and second, the keypress, which basically comes under the heuristics approach.

One such solution is described in this chapter (Rao & Ali, 2015), where a computer vision technique called SURF descriptors (Bay et al., 2006) is used to extract discriminative key point descriptors of both legitimate and suspicious websites, and based on the similarity threshold, a warning for further inspection of the suspicious website is displayed.

Another comparison-based phishing detection application utilizes Contrast Context Histograms (CCH) descriptors (Chen et al., 2009) to compare the similarity degree between suspicious and authentic web pages. In this approach, in step 1, features of suspicious websites are extracted using CCH descriptors and are compared with those stored locally. And in step 2, the decision of phish or not-phish is established based on a pre-defined similarity threshold, which in this case is 0.6.

Along similar lines, where image descriptors of the suspicious websites are compared with some locally stored legitimate website descriptors, is the one which utilizes HOG image descriptors to detect phishing (Bozkir & Sezer, 2016). Basically, HOG features of the highly vulnerable websites' images are extracted, and visual signatures of those websites are stored in a local datastore. And during runtime, the same HOG features of the suspicious websites are extracted, and the similar visual signature of the suspicious website is compared with their legitimate counterpart websites' visual signatures in the local datastore. And based on this comparison, the website is classified as phishing or legitimate.

Machine Learning-Based Techniques

We next discuss the machine learning-based classification mechanism for phishing detection. Similar to the comparison-based approach, features are extracted from website images. However, unlike comparison-based approaches, wherein the extracted features are compared with the locally stored legitimate features, here patterns are extracted from those features using some machine learning algorithms, and a classification model is built, which is used for phishing detection in real time.

One such approach is PhishIRIS (Dalgic et al., 2018), which utilizes MPEG7 (Rayar, 2017) and MPEG7 like Compact Visual Descriptors (CVD), Scalable Colour descriptor (SCD), Colour Layout Descriptor (CLD), CEDD, Fuzzy Colour and Textual Histogram (FCTH) and Joint Composite Descriptors (JCD). Some of the aforementioned descriptors are extracted by the fusion of multiple descriptors, as described in this chapter (Chatzichristofis et al., 2010). It discusses the behavior of Compact Composite Descriptor in Early Fusion, Late Fusion and Distributed Image retrieval.

The aforementioned image descriptors are extracted from the website snapshot, transformed into feature vectors and fed into machine learning algorithms like Support Vector Machine (SVM) and Random Forest (RF) to classify the website as legitimate or phishing.

Dalgic et al. (2018) developed an open-source dataset which comprises website images of 14 different highly phished brands, popularly known as Phish-IRIS (*Phish-IRIS Dataset – A Small Scale Multi-Class Phishing Web Page Screenshots Archive*, n.d.).

Eroğlu et al. (2019) explore GIST and LBP features to determine the brand of the phishing web pages. In this study, GIST and LBP features are extracted and input into machine learning algorithms like SVM, RF and XGB for the classification task. The GIST descriptor focuses on the outline of an object in the image. The LBP descriptor identifies each pixel with two codes and analyses the textures of a local patch by comparing the central pixel to neighboring pixels. Using these two image descriptors, the researchers used two feature extraction schemes: (1) holistic and (2) multi-level patches.

In a holistic scheme, the feature vector is generated using the full website image. And in a multi-level patches scheme, the image is divided into multiple patches like 2×2 and 3×3 patches and features are extracted and fed into three machine learning classifiers built using SVM, Random Forest and XGBoost algorithms. The results are evaluated based on accuracy, false positive rate, true positive rate and F1 score metrics. Among all the iterations on different ML models, GIST with XGBoost appears to be the most accurate and the fastest. Each evaluation takes around 1.5 seconds, which makes this model fit to be deployed as a plugin on a web browser for real-time detection.

Bozkır and Aydos (2019) explore the SIFT (Wu et al., 2013) and DAISY (Tola et al., 2010) features to determine the brand of the phishing web pages. The feature vector extracted via SIFT and DAISY is further fused with the bag of visual words (BOVW) and fed into SVM, XGB and RF classifiers for the classification. SIFT with 400 BOVW fed into XGBoost results in the optimum evaluation metrics of accuracy, TPR, FPR and F1 score.

CHALLENGES IN PHISHING DETECTION USING WEBSITE IMAGES

The major challenges in phishing detection using only website images are:

1) Since phishing websites are built visually similar to their legitimate counterparts, the whole HTML of a legitimate website may be used to build a phishing website. But usually phishers will not do so, because phishing detection mechanisms based on HTML comparison are already in place. Hence, if they do this, they will be caught right at the outset.

2) Storing a huge corpus of legitimate image visual signatures for comparison needs a huge datastore for maintaining and scanning, plus regular updates of such datastore.

3) In order to compare the text-based visual signatures of the website image in question, their legitimate counterparts depend on third-party tools like OCR tools, Google API, and so on.

4) In order to extract the brand of the phishing website, which can be later used to compare the domain with the legitimate website, region of interest and various image invariances have to be factored in to build a machine learning model accordingly.

5) In order to experiment with multiple image descriptors of the website, images will need a huge amount of labeled data and a huge resourcing capacity to build a very advanced neural-network-based classification model, as image processing is computationally expensive.

COMPARISON OF TECHNIQUES

As per the literature reviews, within phishing detection techniques, especially pixel-based approaches, which are the focus of this research, there are usually three different approaches that have been explored.

1) Extracting various website features, including image and text on the websites, and based on some pre-defined rules, where it is decided whether the website in question is phish or not-phish.

2) Extracting image-based features from the website images and creating a visual signature of the website. Based on the comparison result it is decided whether the website in question is phish or not-phish.

3) Extracting image features of the websites and using the transformed features as an input to the machine learning algorithm to develop a classification model, which can classify whether the website in question is phish or not-phish.

SUMMARY OF PHISHING DETECTION USING IMAGE PROCESSING TECHNIQUES

Table 2.1 provides a summary of the previous studies done on phishing detection using website images. In this table, image descriptors extracted and data mining techniques employed for final phishing detection are listed.

Various Experimentations Using CNN

The three high-level approaches we are going to experiment with in this study are traditional CNN, transfer learning and representation learning.

Traditional CNN
In this approach, we will build a custom CNN model with convolution layers and fully connected dense layers.

Transfer Learning
In this approach, learned parameters of CNN architectures till the last fully connected layer are used, and an added softmax layer is added for classification.

Representation Learning
1) Features extracted from the last convolution layer and class balancing using SMOTE.

2) Features extracted from the last convolution layer and class balancing using SMOTE and with horizontal feature fusion.

TABLE 2.1 Study of Past Studies of Phishing Detection Using Image Processing Techniques

RESEARCH	IMAGE DESCRIPTORS USED	AUTHOR AND YEAR	DATA MINING TECHNIQUE	PERFORMANCE MEASURE
Fighting Phishing with Discriminative Key Point Features	Contrast context histogram (CCH)	Chen, Kuan Ta Chen, Jau Yuan Huang, Chun Rong Chen, Chu Song 2009	Passive comparison-based	Accuracy, false negative rate, false positive rate
GoldPhish: Using Images for Content-Based Phishing Analysis	Logo extraction using OCR	Matthew Dunlop, Stephen Groat, David Shelly 2010	Passive comparison- and heuristic-based	False negative rate=2%; false positive rate=0%
Verilogo: Proactive Phishing Detection via Logo Recognition	Logo extraction using SIFT	Ge Wang He Liu 2010	Passive comparison- and heuristic-based	Accuracy=90%
PhishZoo: Detecting Phishing Websites By Looking at Them	Logo extraction using SIFT	Sadia Afroz, Rachel Greenstadt 2011	Passive comparison- and heuristic-based	
A Computer Vision Technique to Detect Phishing Attacks	SURF	Routhu Srinivasa Rao, Syed Taqi Ali 2015	Passive comparison-based	False negative rate=15.23%; false positive rate=20.11%
Use of HOG Descriptors in Phishing Detection Ahmet	HOG	A.S. Bozkir, E.K. Sezer 2016	Passive comparison-based	

(Continued)

TABLE 2.1 (CONTINUED)   Study of Past Studies of Phishing Detection Using Image Processing Techniques

RESEARCH	IMAGE DESCRIPTORS USED	AUTHOR AND YEAR	DATA MINING TECHNIQUE	PERFORMANCE MEASURE
Phish-IRIS: A New Approach for Vision-Based Brand Prediction of Phishing Web Pages via Compact Visual Descriptors	SCD, CLD, CEDD, FCTH, JCD	F.C. Dalgic, A.S. Bozkir, M. Aydos 2018	Machine learning-based SVM, Random Forest	F1 score=90.5%
Brand Recognition of Phishing Web Pages via Global Image Descriptors	GIST, LBP	Esra Eroglu, A.S. Bozkir M. Aydos 2019	Machine learning-based SVM, Random Forest XGBoost	F1 score=88%
Local Image Descriptor-Based Phishing Web Page Recognition as an Open-Set Problem	SIFT, DAISY	A.S. Bozkir M. Aydos 2019	Machine learning-based SVM, Random Forest XGBoost	F1 score=89%
VisualPhishNet: Zero-Day Phishing Website Detection by Visual Similarity	NA	Sahar Abdelnabi Katharina Krombholz Mario Fritz 2020	Deep learning-based VGG16 ResNet50	ROC AUC=98.79%

3) Features extracted from the last convolution layer and class balancing using SMOTE and dimensionality reduction using PCA.

4) Features extracted from the last convolution layer and class balancing using SMOTE and dimensionality reduction using PCA with horizontal and vertical feature fusion.

Summary

Computer vision-based methods for phishing detection have numerous advantages over other traditional approaches. Since they depend on the screenshot of the website, computer vision-based methods are robust web page content manipulation methods used by phishers and are invariant from HTML versions. Most importantly, it works well on zero-hour attacks. In the next chapter, we will build a basic Convolutional Neural Network (CNN) classification model to classify the brand of the website images.

Implementing CNN for Classifying Phishing Websites

3

In the world of computer vision, classifying images into pre-defined classes has solved many complex problem statements. In this process, features extracted from images can be used to train a neural network to classify images. Classifying dogs, cats, airplanes, cars, and so on, are the most common implementations of computer vision. However, the network can be built to classify the brand of the website images. In this chapter, we will build a traditional Convolutional Neural Network (CNN) to classify website images as either phishing or non-phishing using an open dataset.

STRUCTURE

In this chapter, we will cover the following topics:

- Build a CNN model for image classification
- Classify phishing website images to their respective brands
- Define performance metrics

OBJECTIVE

After studying this chapter, you should be able to build a basic convolutional neural network. You should be able to build a neural network to classify

DOI: 10.1201/9781003217381-3

images into pre-defined classes. You will also learn how to validate the model and how to calculate the accuracy of the model. For a classification task, a few more metrics other than accuracy must be calculated to assess the performance of the model, which largely depends on the problem statement.

DATA SELECTION AND PRE-PROCESSING

The Phish-IRIS dataset is generated by Dalgic et al. (2018) and is made publicly available (*Phish-IRIS Dataset – A Small Scale Multi-Class Phishing Web Page Screenshots Archive*, n.d.) for further exploring phishing detection techniques using phishing website images. It is a labeled dataset readily available for research work. The dataset comprises 2852 screenshots of websites containing images from 14 highly phished brands in their respective folders and images from legitimate web pages in one other folder. So overall it is a multi-class dataset with (14 + 1) classes. The data is collected from March to May 2018.

Table 3.1 shows the list of brands whose phishing web page images are present in the dataset along with the information of the number of images for each brand.

TABLE 3.1   PHISH-IRIS Dataset Details

BRAND NAME	TRAINING SAMPLES	TESTING SAMPLES
Adobe	43	27
Alibaba	50	26
Amazon	18	11
Apple	49	15
Bank of America	81	35
Chase Bank	74	37
Dhl	67	42
Dropbox	75	40
Facebook	87	57
Linkedin	24	14
Microsoft	65	53
PayPal	121	93
Wellsfargo	89	45
Yahoo	70	44
Other	400	1000
Total	**1313**	**1539**

The "other" folder contains the images of all the legitimate websites. Since this is not a comparison-based approach, the "other" folder contains images of brands other than the 14 brands chosen for phishing website images. Also, since most websites on the internet are legitimate websites, the addition of this "other" folder makes this dataset an open-set, since the images in this folder have no common color scheme or edge structure that characterizes its own class.

Another important feature of this dataset is that it is not a comparison-based modeling dataset. For example, there is a folder for the "Amazon" brand which contains Amazon phishing website images. There is no folder corresponding to Amazon's legitimate website images. Basically, the model will not be trained to differentiate between a phish Amazon image and a legitimate Amazon image. On the contrary, the other folder contains images of the websites which are not part of those 14 phishing brands.

If there is no "other" folder in the dataset, then it means that this dataset belongs to the 14 brands. With the inclusion of the "other" folder, this dataset becomes an open dataset, meaning this dataset can be used to train a model not only to detect the 14 phishing brands, but also to classify any website as phishing or legitimate.

There are 1313 training and 1539 testing web pages in the dataset, which are already separated into two different folders. Since images of individual brands are stored in the folder named by brand, images are considered as labeled.

The size of the images ranges from 700 pixels to 1280 pixels in terms of both width and height. Hence, there is a need to resize the images and bring them all to the same size format.

As can be seen in Table 3.1, the "other" folder contains far more images than brand-specific images. Also, since it is a multi-class classification problem, class imbalance is visible in the dataset. Hence, there is a need to incorporate class imbalance techniques like SMOTE (Chawla et al., 2002).

CLASSIFICATION USING CNN

At the outset, a traditional CNN application will be designed and built with optimized hyperparameters to produce the best results within the computational limitations, to set a baseline of the performance.

Within this approach, various convolution layers will be built, features from which will be flattened and ingested into densely fully connected layers and trained for building the best classification model.

CNN IMPLEMENTATION

The Phish-IRIS data are structured in such a way that there are two folders: train and val. All images specific to a particular brand are stored in the folder named by the brand. The same structure is followed in both folders.

Let's read the data using Python image-processing libraries.

First, import requires Python libraries.

```
1. import numpy as np
2. import matplotlib.pyplot as plt
3. from glob import glob
4. import os
```

Set the train and the test data path in the filesystem.

```
5.train_path = '../data/phishIRIS/train'
6.test_path = '../data/phishIRIS/val'
```

List all the directories in the train and test folders.

```
7.train_dir = os.listdir(train_path)
8.test_dir = os.listdir(test_path)
9.print(train_dir)
```

```
['apple',
'chase',
'amazon',
'microsoft',
'other',
'alibaba',
'adobe',
'facebook',
'wellsfargo',
'paypal',
'boa',
'dropbox',
'dhl',
'linkedin',
'yahoo']
```

Create a list of all the images with the associated brand (class) in each folder within the training dataset.

```
1.  # Create an empty list to store all image and class
    details
2.  train_data_list = []
3.  # Iterate over every folder within the training
    folder
4.  for brand in train_dir:
5.  # Capture all images within individual folder
6.  all_images = os.listdir(train_path + '/' +brand)
7.  # Iterate over each image in the folder
8.  for image in all_images:
9.  # Append the list with class and image file name
10. train_data_list.append((brand, str(train_path + '/'
    +brand) + '/' + image))
11. # Print the final list created
12. print(train_data_list)
```

```
[('apple', '../data/phishIRIS/train/apple/apple (31).png'),
('apple', '../data/phishIRIS/train/apple/apple (27).png'),
('apple', '../data/phishIRIS/train/apple/apple (6).png'),
('apple', '../data/phishIRIS/train/apple/apple (46).png'),
('apple', '../data/phishIRIS/train/apple/apple (11).png'),
('apple', '../data/phishIRIS/train/apple/apple (10).png'),
('apple', '../data/phishIRIS/train/apple/apple (47).png'),
('apple', '../data/phishIRIS/train/apple/apple (7).png'),
('apple', '../data/phishIRIS/train/apple/apple (26).png'),
('apple', '../data/phishIRIS/train/apple/apple (30).png'),
('apple', '../data/phishIRIS/train/apple/apple (40).png'),
('apple', '../data/phishIRIS/train/apple/apple (17).png'),
('apple', '../data/phishIRIS/train/apple/apple (37).png'),
('apple', '../data/phishIRIS/train/apple/apple (21).png'),
('apple', '../data/phishIRIS/train/apple/apple (1).png'),
('apple', '../data/phishIRIS/train/apple/apple (20).png'),
('apple', '../data/phishIRIS/train/apple/apple (36).png'),
('apple', '../data/phishIRIS/train/apple/apple (16).png'),
('apple', '../data/phishIRIS/train/apple/apple (41).png'),
('apple', '../data/phishIRIS/train/apple/apple (39).png'),
('apple', '../data/phishIRIS/train/apple/apple (15).png'),
('apple', '../data/phishIRIS/train/apple/apple (42).png'),
('apple', '../data/phishIRIS/train/apple/apple (2).png'),
('apple', '../data/phishIRIS/train/apple/apple (23).png'),
('apple', '../data/phishIRIS/train/apple/apple (35).png'),
('apple', '../data/phishIRIS/train/apple/apple (19).png'),
('apple', '../data/phishIRIS/train/apple/apple (18).png'),
('apple', '../data/phishIRIS/train/apple/apple (34).png'),
('apple', '../data/phishIRIS/train/apple/apple (22).png'),
```

Repeat the same exercise for testing the dataset.

```
1.  # Create an empty list to store all image and class
    details
2.  test_data_list = []
3.  # Iterate over every folder within the testing
    folder
4.  for brand in test_dir:
5.  # Capture all images within individual folder
6.  all_images = os.listdir(test_path + '/' +brand)
7.  # Iterate over each image in the folder
8.  for image in all_images:
9.  # Append the list with class and image file name
10. test_data_list.append((brand, str(test_path + '/'
    +brand) + '/' + image))
11. # Print the final list created
12. print(test_data_list)
```

```
[('apple', '../data/phishIRIS/val/apple/apple_test (3).png'),
 ('apple', '../data/phishIRIS/val/apple/apple_test (14).png'),
 ('apple', '../data/phishIRIS/val/apple/apple_test (2).png'),
 ('apple', '../data/phishIRIS/val/apple/apple_test (13).png'),
 ('apple', '../data/phishIRIS/val/apple/apple_test (9).png'),
 ('apple', '../data/phishIRIS/val/apple/apple_test (5).png'),
 ('apple', '../data/phishIRIS/val/apple/apple_test (4).png'),
 ('apple', '../data/phishIRIS/val/apple/apple_test (8).png'),
 ('apple', '../data/phishIRIS/val/apple/apple_test (12).png'),
 ('apple', '../data/phishIRIS/val/apple/apple_test (11).png'),
 ('apple', '../data/phishIRIS/val/apple/apple_test (7).png'),
 ('apple', '../data/phishIRIS/val/apple/apple_test (6).png'),
 ('apple', '../data/phishIRIS/val/apple/apple_test (10).png'),
 ('apple', '../data/phishIRIS/val/apple/apple_test (1).png'),
 ('apple', '../data/phishIRIS/val/apple/apple_test (1).jpg'),
 ('chase', '../data/phishIRIS/val/chase/chase_test (6).png'),
 ('chase', '../data/phishIRIS/val/chase/chase_test (11).jpg'),
 ('chase', '../data/phishIRIS/val/chase/chase_test (11).png'),
 ('chase', '../data/phishIRIS/val/chase/chase_test (6).jpg'),
 ('chase', '../data/phishIRIS/val/chase/chase_test (7).jpg'),
 ('chase', '../data/phishIRIS/val/chase/chase_test (10).png'),
 ('chase', '../data/phishIRIS/val/chase/chase_test (10).jpg'),
 ('chase', '../data/phishIRIS/val/chase/chase_test (7).png'),
 ('chase', '../data/phishIRIS/val/chase/chase_test (17).png'),
 ('chase', '../data/phishIRIS/val/chase/chase_test (21).png'),
```

Capture the number of folders and the number of files within each folder in both the train and test datasets.

```
1.  # No of files
2.  train_image_files = glob(train_path + '/*/*.*')
3.  test_image_files = glob(test_path + '/*/*.*')
```

```
4. # No of classes
5. folders = glob(train_path + '/*')
6. print(len(train_image_files))
```

1313

```
7. print(len(test_image_files))
```

1539

```
8. print(len(folders))
```

15

As can be seen, there is a total of 15 folders in the dataset, which means there is a total of 15 brands for which image files are captured. There is a total of 1313 images in the training dataset and 1539 images in the testing dataset.

Now, let's create pandas DataFrame with class and image file details for better processing of the data.

Training and testing DataFrames.

```
1. df_train = pd.DataFrame(data=train_data_list,
   columns=['brand', 'image'])
2. df_test = pd.DataFrame(data=test_data_list,
   columns=['brand', 'image'])
3. df_train.head()
```

	brand	image
0	apple	../data/phishIRIS/train/apple/apple (31).png
1	apple	../data/phishIRIS/train/apple/apple (27).png
2	apple	../data/phishIRIS/train/apple/apple (6).png
3	apple	../data/phishIRIS/train/apple/apple (46).png
4	apple	../data/phishIRIS/train/apple/apple (11).png

Set the image size to 128×128 pixels.

```
1. img_rows = 128
2. img_cols = 128
3. channel = 3
```

Now, let's extract the pixel values from the images and store them into a numpy array. Further, store the image arrays and image labels into two separate Python lists for further processing.

Training data transformation.

```
1.  # Create empty list to store image arrays and image
    class
2.  train_images = []
3.  train_labels = []
4.
5.  # Iterate over each image in the DataFrame
6.  for f in list(df_train['image']):
7.      # Convert the image into an array
8.      img = cv2.imread(f)
9.      # Resize the image to a pre-defined image size
10.     img = cv2.resize(img, (img_rows, img_cols))
11.     # Append the image array into the list
12.     train_images.append(img)
13. # Transform the image array to a numpy type
14. train_images = np.array(train_images)
15. # Convert the DataFrame brand column into a list
16. train_labels=list(df_train["brand"])
17. # Print the list shape
18. train_images.shape
```

Following is the final shape of the training dataset:

```
(1313, 128, 128, 3)
```

The shape of the training dataset implies that there are 1313 image arrays of image size of 128×128 and 3 channels (RGB).

Testing data transformation.

```
1.  # Create empty list to store image arrays and image
    class
2.  test_images = []
3.  test_labels = []
4.
5.  # Iterate over each image in the DataFrame
6.  for f in list(df_test['image']):
7.      # Convert the image into an array
8.      img = cv2.imread(f)
9.      # Resize the image to a pre-defined image size
10.     img = cv2.resize(img, (img_rows, img_cols))
11.     # Append the image array into the list
12.     test_images.append(img)
```

```
13. # Transform the image array to a numpy type
14. test_images = np.array(test_images)
15. # Convert the DataFrame brand column into a list
16. test_labels=list(df_test["brand"])
17. # Print the list shape
18. test_images.shape
```

Following is the final shape of the testing dataset.

```
(1539, 128, 128, 3)
```

The shape of the testing dataset implies that there are 1313 image arrays of image size of 128×128 and 3 channels (RGB).

Normalize the pixel values.

```
1. # convert from integers to floats
2. trainX = train_images.astype('float32')
3. testX = test_images.astype('float32')
4. # normalize to range 0-1
5. trainX = trainX / 255.0
6. testX = testX / 255.0
```

Plot a sample image after normalizing the pixel values (Figure 3.1).

```
1. plt.imshow(trainX[0])
```

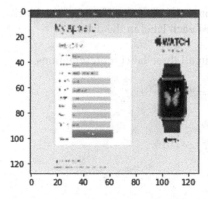

FIGURE 3.1   Sample image output.

Label Encoding for Machine Learning Classifier

Since machine learning classifiers only work with numerical label values, we used Python library sklearn's LabelEncoder module to convert the categorical labels into numerically encoded label arrays.

Label encoding Python implementation:

```
1. from sklearn.preprocessing import LabelEncoder
2. le = LabelEncoder()
3. le.fit(train_labels)
4. trainY_le = le.transform(train_labels)
5. testY_le = le.transform(test_labels)
```

One Hot Encoding for Deep Learning Classifier

Since deep learning classifiers only work with one-hot encoded labels, we used Python library sklearn's LabelBinarizer module to convert the labels into one-hot encoded label arrays.

Label Binarizer Python implementation.

```
1. from sklearn.preprocessing import LabelBinarizer
2. lb = LabelBinarizer()
3. lb.fit(train_labels)
4. trainY_lb = lb.transform(train_labels)
5. testY_lb = lb.transform(test_labels)
```

Table 3.2 demonstrates the numerically encoded label values and one-hot encoded labels against each label in the dataset.

Print a sample label in all three label representations.

```
1.print(train_labels[0])
```

apple

```
2.print(trainY_le[0])
```

3

```
3.print(testY_lb[0])
```

[0 0 0 1 0 0 0 0 0 0 0 0 0 0 0]

TABLE 3.2 Encodings for Machine Learning and Deep Learning Models

LABEL	LABEL ENCODING	ONE-HOT ENCODING
Adobe	0	100000000000000
Alibaba	1	010000000000000
Amazon	2	001000000000000
Apple	3	000100000000000
Boa	4	000010000000000
Chase	5	000001000000000
Dhl	6	000000100000000
Dropbox	7	000000010000000
Facebook	8	000000001000000
Linkedin	9	000000000100000
Microsoft	10	000000000010000
Other	11	000000000001000
PayPal	12	000000000000100
Wellsfargo	13	000000000000010
Yahoo	14	000000000000001

PERFORMANCE METRICS

This is a multi-classification problem where we intend to classify brands of the 14 phishing websites and one class for legitimate websites.

To derive the performance metrics of a multi-class classification problem, let's first understand the performance metrics for any binary classification problem.

For the binary classification task, we will consider images in all the brand folders as "phish", meaning positive class, and images in the "other" folder as "not-phish", meaning negative class.

Upon building a confusion matrix for binary classification results, we can see all the possible combinations for the two-class classification (binary) problem as depicted in Table 3.3.

To understand this, let's first understand TN, TP, FN and FP in the phishing detection context.

TN (True Negative) – Number of "not-phish" (legitimate) websites classified as "not-phish".

FN (False Negative) – Number of "not-phish" (legitimate) websites classified as "phish".

TABLE 3.3 Confusion Matrix for Binary Classification

	PREDICTED PHISHING	PREDICTED LEGITIMATE
Actual phishing	TP	FN
Actual legitimate	FP	TN

FP (False Positive) – Number of "phish" websites classified as "not-phish" (legitimate).
TP (True Positive) – Number of "phish" websites classified as "phish".

For the phishing detection binary classification, it would be important to consider the following:

1) Rate of correct classifications, that is, phishing websites classified as "phish" and legitimate websites classified as "not-phish", which as per definition is the accuracy of the classifier.
2) Rate of phishing websites that the classifier is able to classify among the total phishing websites in the dataset, which as per the definition is TPR.
3) Rate of legitimate websites that the classifier classifies as "phish", which as per definition is FPR.

Hence, for such kinds of binary classification, we need to consider accuracy, TPR, FPR and F1 score.

Accuracy means how accurate is the classifier to classify phishing websites as "phish" class and legitimate websites as "not-phish" class. Accuracy is the ratio of all the correct classifications against the total images in the dataset.

$$ACC = \frac{TP + TN}{TP + TN + FP + FN}$$

TPR is the measure of the number of phishing websites correctly classified as "phish" among the total phishing images in the dataset. TPR is also termed as Recall.

$$TPR = \frac{TP}{TP + FN}$$

FPR is the measure of the number of legitimate websites classified as "phish" out of the total legitimate website images in the dataset.

$$FPR = \frac{FP}{FP + TN}$$

Another important performance metric that we will calculate here will be F1 score. F1 score is the harmonic mean of Recall (REC) and Precision (PRE).

$$PRE = \frac{TP}{TP + FP}$$

$$REC = TPR = \frac{TP}{FN + TP}$$

$$F1 = 2 \cdot \frac{PRE \cdot REC}{PRE + REC}$$

In case of multi-class classification, the definition of all the metrics remains the same; however, the way they have to be inferred is different.

Precision in the multi-class context would mean the number of web pages detected as a particular class, which actually belongs to that class. No other class is detected for that phishing brand. This would not be a good measure in case of detecting phishing websites, because it may miss out on detecting a lot of phishing websites as "phish", but still would show a high value. For example, in the below confusion matrix, out of 27 Adobe web pages, only 11 web pages are classified correctly.

For the confusion matrix depicted in Figure 3.2, precision for "Adobe" is 100% as all the websites predicted as "Adobe" are actually Adobe, but there are many Adobe web pages that are detected as other brands. So, ideally the model does a very poor job detecting the right brand of the website. However, whatever brand the model detects will be almost correct.

Recall, on the other hand, actually tells, for a given brand, how many of their web pages are detected correctly. For example, in the confusion matrix depicted in Figure 3.3, out of 27 Adobe web pages, 21 web pages are classified correctly.

Also, the mathematical formula for the calculation of the FP, FN, TP and TN for the multi-class classification through the values in the confusion matrix will be different from that of the binary classification. For the binary classification, values will be available in the respective cell of the confusion matrix as shown in Table 3.3. However, for the multi-class classification, those values will be calculated using Python numpy library as below:

$$FP = cnf\_matrix.sum(axis=0) - np.diag(cnf\_matrix)$$

As per the formula for calculating FP, first all the images predicted as "Adobe" are to be calculated. For example, as per the confusion matrix in Figure 3.3, we first add all the images which are predicted as "Adobe", which is 27. Then

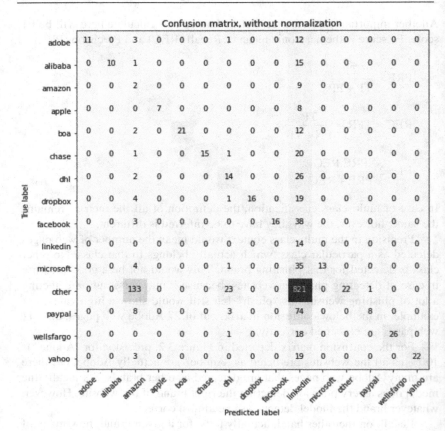

Confusion matrix, without normalization

True label	adobe	alibaba	amazon	apple	boa	chase	dhl	dropbox	facebook	linkedin	microsoft	other	paypal	wellsfargo	yahoo
adobe	11	0	3	0	0	0	1	0	0	12	0	0	0	0	0
alibaba	0	10	1	0	0	0	0	0	0	15	0	0	0	0	0
amazon	0	0	2	0	0	0	0	0	0	9	0	0	0	0	0
apple	0	0	0	7	0	0	0	0	0	8	0	0	0	0	0
boa	0	0	2	0	21	0	0	0	0	12	0	0	0	0	0
chase	0	0	1	0	0	15	1	0	0	20	0	0	0	0	0
dhl	0	0	2	0	0	0	14	0	0	26	0	0	0	0	0
dropbox	0	0	4	0	0	0	1	16	0	19	0	0	0	0	0
facebook	0	0	3	0	0	0	0	0	16	38	0	0	0	0	0
linkedin	0	0	0	0	0	0	0	0	0	14	0	0	0	0	0
microsoft	0	0	4	0	0	0	1	0	0	35	13	0	0	0	0
other	0	0	133	0	0	0	23	0	0	821	0	22	1	0	0
paypal	0	0	8	0	0	0	3	0	0	74	0	0	8	0	0
wellsfargo	0	0	0	0	0	0	1	0	0	18	0	0	0	26	0
yahoo	0	0	3	0	0	0	0	0	0	19	0	0	0	0	22

Predicted label

FIGURE 3.2 Confusion matrix example 1.

we need to subtract the number of images that are actually "Adobe", which is 21. Hence, FP for "Adobe" class is 27 − 21 = 6. This actually means that six images are predicted as "Adobe", but are not. And similarly, FP for all the other classes is calculated.

$$FN = cnf\_matrix.sum(axis = 1) - np.diag(cnf\_matrix)$$

As per the above formula for FN, we need to first calculate the number of all the images that are actually "Adobe", which as per the confusion matrix in Figure 3.3 is 27. But as can be seen in the confusion matrix, out of the 27 actual "Adobe" images, 5 images are predicted as "other" class and one image is predicted as "PayPal" class.

$$TP = np.diag(cnf\_matrix)$$

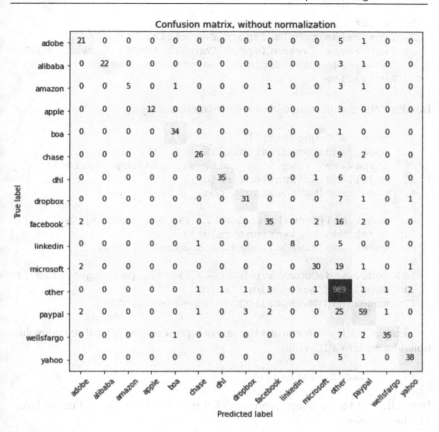

FIGURE 3.3   Confusion matrix example 2.

TP basically means the number of images that were predicted correctly. As can be seen in the confusion matrix in Figure 3.11, all the images in the diagonal of the matrix are the ones that are predicted correctly.

$$TN = cnf\_matrix.sum() - (FP + FN + TP)$$

Further, the formula to calculate accuracy, precision, recall and so on will remain the same as in the binary classification.

BUILDING A CONVOLUTIONAL NEURAL NETWORK MODEL

Import required libraries.

```
1. import tensorflow as tf
2. from keras.models import Sequential
3. from keras.layers import Convolution2D, MaxPooling2D,
   Dense, Flatten, Dropout, BatchNormalization,
   Activation
```

Build a CNN architecture with three convolutional layers.

```
1.  model = Sequential()
2.  model.add(Convolution2D(32, (3, 3), input_
    shape=(img_rows, img_cols, 3), padding='valid'))
3.  model.add(Activation('relu'))
4.  model.add(MaxPooling2D(pool_size=(2, 2)))
5.
6.  model.add(Convolution2D(32, (3, 3), padding='valid'))
7.  model.add(Activation('relu'))
8.  model.add(MaxPooling2D(pool_size=(2, 2)))
9.
10. model.add(Convolution2D(64, (3, 3), padding='valid'))
11. model.add(Activation('relu'))
12. model.add(MaxPooling2D(pool_size=(2, 2)))
```

Flatten the layer to convert the image representation after three convolutional layers into a 1D vector.

```
13.model.add(Flatten())
```

Ingest the 1D vector image representation into a fully connected dense layer for classification.

```
14. model.add(Dense(64))
15. model.add(Activation('relu'))
16. model.add(Dropout(0.5))
```

Finally, add an output layer with 15 neurons for 15 classes for classification.

```
17. model.add(Dense(15))
18. model.add(Activation('softmax'))
```

Compile the model against accuracy, precision and recall performance metrics.

```
19. model.compile(loss='categorical_crossentropy',
20. optimizer='rmsprop',
21. metrics=['accuracy', tf.keras.metrics.Precision(),
    tf.keras.metrics.Recall()])
```

Print the model architecture summary.

```
1. model.summary()
```

```
Model: "sequential"
_____
Layer (type)                  Output Shape               Param #
=================================================================
conv2d (Conv2D)               (None, 126, 126, 32)       896
_____
activation (Activation)       (None, 126, 126, 32)       0
_____
max_pooling2d (MaxPooling2D)  (None, 63, 63, 32)         0
_____
conv2d_1 (Conv2D)             (None, 61, 61, 32)         9248
_____
activation_1 (Activation)     (None, 61, 61, 32)         0
_____
max_pooling2d_1 (MaxPooling2  (None, 30, 30, 32)         0
_____
conv2d_2 (Conv2D)             (None, 28, 28, 64)         18496
_____
activation_2 (Activation)     (None, 28, 28, 64)         0
_____
max_pooling2d_2 (MaxPooling2  (None, 14, 14, 64)         0
_____
flatten (Flatten)             (None, 12544)              0
_____
dense (Dense)                 (None, 64)                 802880
_____
activation_3 (Activation)     (None, 64)                 0
_____
dropout (Dropout)             (None, 64)                 0
_____
dense_1 (Dense)               (None, 15)                 975
_____
activation_4 (Activation)     (None, 15)                 0
=================================================================
Total params: 832,495
Trainable params: 832,495
Non-trainable params: 0
_____
```

Set the epochs and batch size for the model training.

```
1. epochs = 25
2. batch_size = 128
```

Train the model.

```
3. history = model.fit(trainX, trainY_lb, batch_size =
   batch_size, epochs = epochs, verbose = 1, validation_
   data = (testX, testY_lb))
```

```
Epoch 15/25
11/11 [==============================] - 7s 682ms/step - loss: 1.1448 - accuracy: 0.6294 - precision: 0.8044 - reca
ll: 0.3297 - val_loss: 0.8841 - val_accuracy: 0.7524 - val_precision: 0.8085 - val_recall: 0.3383
Epoch 16/25
11/11 [==============================] - 7s 684ms/step - loss: 1.0012 - accuracy: 0.6775 - precision: 0.8113 - reca
ll: 0.3438 - val_loss: 0.8913 - val_accuracy: 0.7537 - val_precision: 0.8143 - val_recall: 0.3523
Epoch 17/25
11/11 [==============================] - 7s 687ms/step - loss: 1.0248 - accuracy: 0.6538 - precision: 0.8153 - reca
ll: 0.3567 - val_loss: 0.8175 - val_accuracy: 0.7687 - val_precision: 0.8181 - val_recall: 0.3666
Epoch 18/25
11/11 [==============================] - 7s 686ms/step - loss: 0.9717 - accuracy: 0.6791 - precision: 0.8181 - reca
ll: 0.3716 - val_loss: 0.9353 - val_accuracy: 0.7238 - val_precision: 0.8194 - val_recall: 0.3788
Epoch 19/25
11/11 [==============================] - 7s 686ms/step - loss: 0.9575 - accuracy: 0.6834 - precision: 0.8198 - reca
ll: 0.3825 - val_loss: 0.8350 - val_accuracy: 0.7518 - val_precision: 0.8216 - val_recall: 0.3900
Epoch 20/25
11/11 [==============================] - 7s 694ms/step - loss: 0.8177 - accuracy: 0.7388 - precision: 0.8227 - reca
ll: 0.3946 - val_loss: 0.7160 - val_accuracy: 0.8090 - val_precision: 0.8261 - val_recall: 0.4037
Epoch 21/25
11/11 [==============================] - 7s 688ms/step - loss: 0.7469 - accuracy: 0.7488 - precision: 0.8274 - reca
ll: 0.4088 - val_loss: 0.7844 - val_accuracy: 0.8018 - val_precision: 0.8303 - val_recall: 0.4171
Epoch 22/25
11/11 [==============================] - 7s 683ms/step - loss: 0.7546 - accuracy: 0.7481 - precision: 0.8308 - reca
ll: 0.4216 - val_loss: 0.7111 - val_accuracy: 0.8031 - val_precision: 0.8332 - val_recall: 0.4292
Epoch 23/25
11/11 [==============================] - 7s 686ms/step - loss: 0.6669 - accuracy: 0.7729 - precision: 0.8341 - reca
ll: 0.4340 - val_loss: 0.7422 - val_accuracy: 0.8005 - val_precision: 0.8360 - val_recall: 0.4413
Epoch 24/25
11/11 [==============================] - 7s 687ms/step - loss: 0.5952 - accuracy: 0.8030 - precision: 0.8375 - reca
ll: 0.4456 - val_loss: 1.2389 - val_accuracy: 0.7661 - val_precision: 0.8390 - val_recall: 0.4537
Epoch 25/25
11/11 [==============================] - 7s 686ms/step - loss: 0.8881 - accuracy: 0.7168 - precision: 0.8368 - reca
ll: 0.4568 - val_loss: 0.7675 - val_accuracy: 0.7979 - val_precision: 0.8380 - val_recall: 0.4633
```

Compare the predicted labels with actual labels.

```
4. y_pred = model.predict_classes(testX)
5. print("Actual Labels : ", testY_le)
6. print("Predicted Labels : ", y_pred)
```

```
Actual Labels : [ 3 3 3 ... 14 14 14]
Predicted Labels : [11 11 11 ... 14 14 14]
```

Build a classification report.

```
7. print('Classification Report')
8. print(classification_report(testY_le, y_pred,
   target_names=list(np.unique(test_labels))))
```

```
Classification Report
              precision    recall  f1-score   support

       adobe       1.00      0.63      0.77        27
      alibaba       0.91      0.77      0.83        26
       amazon       0.00      0.00      0.00        11
        apple       1.00      0.53      0.70        15
          boa       0.78      0.83      0.81        35
        chase       0.42      0.57      0.48        37
          dhl       0.57      0.88      0.69        42
      dropbox       0.58      0.65      0.61        40
     facebook       0.68      0.60      0.64        57
     linkedin       1.00      0.29      0.44        14
    microsoft       0.90      0.49      0.63        53
        other       0.84      0.91      0.88      1000
       paypal       0.64      0.40      0.49        93
   wellsfargo       0.97      0.71      0.82        45
        yahoo       0.63      0.66      0.64        44

     accuracy                           0.80      1539
    macro avg       0.73      0.59      0.63      1539
 weighted avg       0.80      0.80      0.79      1539
```

Since data are unevenly distributed among the classes, the macro average from the classification report gives better performance metrics. As can be seen from the classification report, the macro average for precision is 69%, for recall is 58% and for accuracy is 61%.

Build a confusion matrix for better visibility of predicted and actual classes.

Reusable function to generate and plot the confusion matrix.

```
1.  from __future__ import print_function, division
2.  from builtins import range, input
3.  import itertools
4.  import numpy as np
5.  import matplotlib.pyplot as plt
6.  from matplotlib.pyplot import figure
7.
8.
9.  def plot_confusion_matrix(cm, classes,
10. normalize=False,
11. title='Confusion matrix',
12. cmap=plt.cm.Blues):
13. """
14. This function prints and plots the confusion matrix.
15. Normalization can be applied by setting
    `normalize=True`.
16. """
17. if normalize:
18. cm = cm.astype('float') / cm.sum(axis=1)[:, np.newaxis]
19. print("Normalized confusion matrix")
20. else:
21. print('Confusion matrix, without normalization')
22.
23. figure(num=None, figsize=(8, 6), dpi=80,
    facecolor='w', edgecolor='k')
24. plt.imshow(cm, interpolation='nearest', cmap=cmap)
25. plt.title(title)
26. plt.colorbar()
27. tick_marks = np.arange(len(classes))
28. plt.xticks(tick_marks, classes, rotation=45)
29. plt.yticks(tick_marks, classes)
30.
31. fmt = '.2f' if normalize else 'd'
32. thresh = cm.max() / 2.
33. for i, j in itertools.product(range(cm.shape[0]),
    range(cm.shape[1])):
34. plt.text(j, i, format(cm[i, j], fmt),
35. horizontalalignment="center",
```

```
36. color="white" if cm[i, j] > thresh else "black")
37. #plt.figure(figsize=(10,10))
38. plt.tight_layout()
39. plt.ylabel('True label')
40. plt.xlabel('Predicted label')
41. plt.show()
```

Create and plot a confusion matrix (Figure 3.4).

```
1. cm=confusion_matrix(testY_le, y_pred)
2. plot_confusion_matrix(cm, list(np.unique(test_
   labels)), title='Confusion matrix')
```

Summary

In this chapter, we have built a simple convolutional neural network, trained the model using a training dataset and validated the model using a test dataset. A simple and plain CNN model is able to achieve nearly 80% accuracy. Further, in subsequent chapters, we will use state-of-the-art CNN architectures to build a model using the Phish-IRIS dataset and the transfer learning approach.

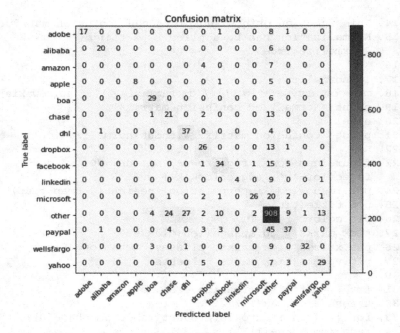

FIGURE 3.4 Confusion matrix for the test dataset.

Transfer Learning Approach in Phishing Detection

4

Building a basic neural network from scratch is a good way to define baseline accuracy. However, we need to improve the network by using a more complicated and deeper architecture. Alternatively, we can use previously defined architectures that have already proved their efficacy in image classification, with the architectures usually applied on image datasets like imagenet, coco, etc. Through the approach of transfer learning, you can utilize such previously built architectures and retrain the model for your specific dataset. Additionally, you can choose not to retrain the model and instead just use the previously learned weights and biases.

STRUCTURE

In this chapter, the following topics will be covered:

- Classification using transfer learning
- Python implementation of transfer learning
- Performance assessment of CNN models

DOI: 10.1201/9781003217381-4

OBJECTIVE

After studying this chapter, you should be able to understand what transfer learning is, and how it's important to use previously discovered neural networks architectures and/or their learned parameters. You will also see the implementation of Python for this purpose. Assessing the performance of the model will let you choose the most appropriate CNN architecture for your problem statement.

CLASSIFICATION USING TRANSFER LEARNING

Transfer learning techniques allow reuse of already trained CNN applications to build a new model with different datasets. Basically, the whole architecture of the already built CNN application is reused, along with trained parameters such as weights, biases, kernels, and so on, without the need for retraining them for a new custom image dataset. This reduces the computational requirement of building a CNN application, and also allows the user to use tried-and-tested learned parameters for obtaining optimum results from a different set of images.

Transfer the Learning up to the Last Fully Connected Layer

In this approach, the transfer learning technique is utilized to classify images. As per Figure 4.1, trained images from the Phish-IRIS dataset are ingested into the CNN application using the transfer learning technique, with the final classification layer being replaced for classifying it among the 15 classes (Figure 4.1).

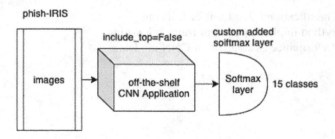

FIGURE 4.1 Transfer learning end-to-end flow.

TRANSFER LEARNING IMPLEMENTATION IN PYTHON

Keras library comes with APIs to include various CNN architectures for a quick implementation of transfer learning in Python. Table 4.1 lists the API import statement for the CNN architectures.
Import required libraries.

```
1. from keras.applications.densenet import DenseNet201,
   preprocess_input
2. from keras.preprocessing import image
3. from keras.preprocessing.image import
   ImageDataGenerator
4. from keras.models import Model
```

Set the hyper-parameters and image size details.

```
5. img_rows=224
6. img_cols=224
7. channel=3
8. epochs=25
9. batch_size=32
```

Load a DenseNet model without the dense layer, which is also called classifier.

```
10. DenseNet201 = DenseNet201(input_shape=[img_rows,
    img_cols, channel], weights='imagenet',
    include_top=False)
```

Basically, this step creates the model architecture similar to the DenseNet201 architecture. Further, the trained weights on "imagenet" are also borrowed. Finally, with "include_top=False", the final dense layer is eliminated from the DenseNet201 architecture.
Now, the layers in the newly created architecture are made non-trainable.

```
11. for layer in DenseNet201.layers:
12. layer.trainable = False
```

By making the layers of the model non-trainable, during the model training process, weights associated with these layers will not be updated, and the weights borrowed from "imagenet" will be used for the final model. This will reduce the training computational requirements drastically.

TABLE 4.1   Keras API Import Statements for CNN Architectures

ARCHITECTURE	KERAS API
Xception	from keras.applications.xception import Xception
VGG16	from keras.applications.vgg16 import VGG16
VGG19	from keras.applications.vgg19 import VGG19
ResNet50	from keras.applications.resnet50 import ResNet50
ResNet101	from keras.applications.resnet import ResNet101
ResNet152	from keras.applications.resnet import ResNet152
ResNet50V2	from keras.applications.resnet_v2 import ResNet50V2
ResNet101V2	from keras.applications.resnet_v2 import ResNet101V2
ResNet152V2	from keras.applications.resnet_v2 import ResNet152V2
InceptionV3	from keras.applications.inception_v3 import InceptionV3
InceptionResNetV2	from keras.applications.inception_resnet_v2 import InceptionResNetV2
MobileNet	from keras.applications.mobilenet import MobileNet
MobileNetV2	from keras.applications.mobilenet_v2 import MobileNetV2
DenseNet121	from keras.applications.densenet import DenseNet121
DenseNet169	from keras.applications.densenet import DenseNet169
DenseNet201	from keras.applications.densenet import DenseNet201

Now, flatten the convolutional layer and convert the image representations into a 1D vector.

```
13. x = Flatten()(DenseNet201.output)
```

Finally, a dense layer is added to the architecture, with the number of output neurons equal to the number of folders in the dataset, which is equal to the number of classes. Softmax activation is used since it's a multi-class classification problem.

```
14. prediction = Dense(len(folders),
    activation='softmax')(x)
```

Create a model object with input as DenseNet201 model input, and output as the prediction layer output.

```
15. model_tl = Model(inputs=DenseNet201.input,
    outputs=prediction)
```

Look at the final model summary.

```
16. model_tl.summary()
```

Since DenseNet is a very deep model, only the last few layers of the model and the trainable parameter description are displayed.

conv5_block31_1_bn (BatchNormal	(None, 7, 7, 128)	512	conv5_block31_1_conv[0][0]
conv5_block31_1_relu (Activatio	(None, 7, 7, 128)	0	conv5_block31_1_bn[0][0]
conv5_block31_2_conv (Conv2D)	(None, 7, 7, 32)	36864	conv5_block31_1_relu[0][0]
conv5_block31_concat (Concatena	(None, 7, 7, 1888)	0	conv5_block30_concat[0][0] conv5_block31_2_conv[0][0]
conv5_block32_0_bn (BatchNormal	(None, 7, 7, 1888)	7552	conv5_block31_concat[0][0]
conv5_block32_0_relu (Activatio	(None, 7, 7, 1888)	0	conv5_block32_0_bn[0][0]
conv5_block32_1_conv (Conv2D)	(None, 7, 7, 128)	241664	conv5_block32_0_relu[0][0]
conv5_block32_1_bn (BatchNormal	(None, 7, 7, 128)	512	conv5_block32_1_conv[0][0]
conv5_block32_1_relu (Activatio	(None, 7, 7, 128)	0	conv5_block32_1_bn[0][0]
conv5_block32_2_conv (Conv2D)	(None, 7, 7, 32)	36864	conv5_block32_1_relu[0][0]
conv5_block32_concat (Concatena	(None, 7, 7, 1920)	0	conv5_block31_concat[0][0] conv5_block32_2_conv[0][0]
bn (BatchNormalization)	(None, 7, 7, 1920)	7680	conv5_block32_concat[0][0]
relu (Activation)	(None, 7, 7, 1920)	0	bn[0][0]
flatten_3 (Flatten)	(None, 94080)	0	relu[0][0]
dense_4 (Dense)	(None, 15)	1411215	flatten_3[0][0]

```
Total params: 19,733,199
Trainable params: 1,411,215
Non-trainable params: 18,321,984
```

It can be seen that the total parameters in the model are 19,733,199, but the trainable parameters are only 14,11,215. This is because other than the last dense layer, all other layers are non-trainable.

Compile the model using optimizer and loss function, and define the performance metrics as accuracy, precision and recall.

```
17. model_tl.compile(
18. loss='categorical_crossentropy',
19. optimizer='rmsprop',
```

```
20. metrics=['accuracy', tf.keras.metrics.Precision(),
    tf.keras.metrics.Recall()]
21.)
```

Create an instance of an image generator of image augmentation.

```
22. gen = ImageDataGenerator(
23. rotation_range=20,
24. width_shift_range=0.1,
25. height_shift_range=0.1,
26. shear_range=0.1,
27. zoom_range=0.2,
28. horizontal_flip=True,
29. vertical_flip=True,
30. preprocessing_function=preprocess_input
31.)
```

Get label mappings that can be used later for building the confusion matrix.

```
32. test_gen = gen.flow_from_directory(test_path,
    target_size=[img_rows, img_cols])
33. print(test_gen.class_indices)
34. labels = [None] * len(test_gen.class_indices)
35. for k, v in test_gen.class_indices.items():
36. labels[v] = k
```

```
Found 1539 images belonging to 15 classes.
```

```
{'adobe': 0, 'alibaba': 1, 'amazon': 2, 'apple': 3,
'boa': 4, 'chase': 5, 'dhl': 6, 'dropbox': 7,
'facebook': 8, 'linkedin': 9, 'microsoft': 10, 'other':
11, 'paypal': 12, 'wellsfargo': 13, 'yahoo': 14}
```

A sample augmented image.

```
37. for x, y in test_gen:
38. print("min:", x[0].min(), "max:", x[0].max())
39. plt.title(labels[np.argmax(y[0])])
40. plt.imshow(x[0])
41. plt.show()
42. break
```

Create a train generator (Figures 4.2 and 4.3).

```
43. train_generator = gen.flow_from_directory(
44. train_path,
45. target_size=[img_rows, img_cols],
```

min: -2.117904 max: 2.64

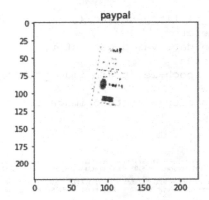

FIGURE 4.2 Sample 1 augmented image.

min: -2.1168218 max: 2.64

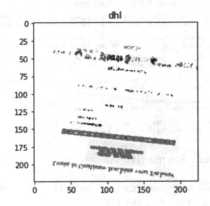

FIGURE 4.3 Sample 2 augmented image.

```
46. shuffle=True,
47. batch_size=batch_size,
48.)
```

Create a validation generator.

```
49. valid_generator = gen.flow_from_directory(
50. test_path,
51. target_size=[img_rows, img_cols],
52. shuffle=True,
53. batch_size=batch_size,
54.)
```

Train the model.

```
55. r = model_tl.fit_generator(
56. train_generator,
57. validation_data=valid_generator,
58. epochs=epochs,
59. steps_per_epoch=len(train_image_files) //
    batch_size,
60. validation_steps=len(test_image_files) //
    batch_size,
61.)
```

```
Epoch 15/25
41/41 [==============================] - 212s 5s/step - loss: 1.4881 - accuracy: 0.8696 - precision: 0.8702 - recal
l: 0.8689 - val_loss: 8.9683 - val_accuracy: 0.5586 - val_precision: 0.5590 - val_recall: 0.5579
Epoch 16/25
41/41 [==============================] - 211s 5s/step - loss: 1.8572 - accuracy: 0.8407 - precision: 0.8414 - recal
l: 0.8407 - val_loss: 3.3777 - val_accuracy: 0.7812 - val_precision: 0.7811 - val_recall: 0.7806
Epoch 17/25
41/41 [==============================] - 215s 5s/step - loss: 1.5743 - accuracy: 0.8735 - precision: 0.8735 - recal
l: 0.8735 - val_loss: 3.0050 - val_accuracy: 0.8190 - val_precision: 0.8195 - val_recall: 0.8190
Epoch 18/25
41/41 [==============================] - 209s 5s/step - loss: 1.7609 - accuracy: 0.8610 - precision: 0.8616 - recal
l: 0.8603 - val_loss: 2.5394 - val_accuracy: 0.8464 - val_precision: 0.8469 - val_recall: 0.8464
Epoch 19/25
41/41 [==============================] - 210s 5s/step - loss: 1.8618 - accuracy: 0.8439 - precision: 0.8439 - recal
l: 0.8439 - val_loss: 3.6078 - val_accuracy: 0.8346 - val_precision: 0.8357 - val_recall: 0.8346
Epoch 20/25
41/41 [==============================] - 213s 5s/step - loss: 1.3423 - accuracy: 0.8868 - precision: 0.8882 - recal
l: 0.8868 - val_loss: 3.2787 - val_accuracy: 0.7982 - val_precision: 0.7986 - val_recall: 0.7975
Epoch 21/25
41/41 [==============================] - 207s 5s/step - loss: 1.3486 - accuracy: 0.8751 - precision: 0.8750 - recal
l: 0.8743 - val_loss: 3.0516 - val_accuracy: 0.8151 - val_precision: 0.8166 - val_recall: 0.8145
Epoch 22/25
41/41 [==============================] - 208s 5s/step - loss: 1.6037 - accuracy: 0.8759 - precision: 0.8772 - recal
l: 0.8759 - val_loss: 2.8348 - val_accuracy: 0.8457 - val_precision: 0.8473 - val_recall: 0.8451
Epoch 23/25
41/41 [==============================] - 205s 5s/step - loss: 1.2933 - accuracy: 0.8985 - precision: 0.9013 - recal
l: 0.8985 - val_loss: 3.1444 - val_accuracy: 0.8255 - val_precision: 0.8264 - val_recall: 0.8242
Epoch 24/25
41/41 [==============================] - 202s 5s/step - loss: 1.3513 - accuracy: 0.8759 - precision: 0.8765 - recal
l: 0.8751 - val_loss: 3.3958 - val_accuracy: 0.8307 - val_precision: 0.8313 - val_recall: 0.8307
Epoch 25/25
41/41 [==============================] - 209s 5s/step - loss: 1.2913 - accuracy: 0.8954 - precision: 0.8954 - recal
l: 0.8954 - val_loss: 3.4845 - val_accuracy: 0.7923 - val_precision: 0.7939 - val_recall: 0.7923
```

Create and plot a confusion matrix.

```
62. valid_cm = get_confusion_matrix(test_path,
    len(test_image_files))
63. plot_confusion_matrix(valid_cm, labels,
    title='Validation confusion matrix')
```

For this experiment, we used the below hyperparameters to train the model (Figure 4.4):

Epochs – 50
Optimizer – Adam

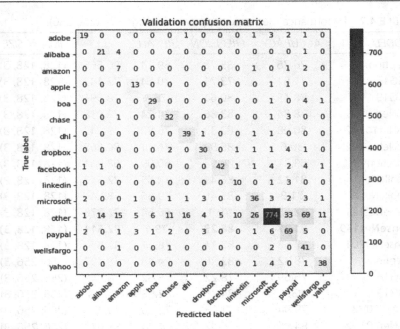

FIGURE 4.4 Confusion matrix for the test dataset.

Learning_rate – 0.0001
Loss – "categorical_crossentropy"
Classes – 15

After the model is trained using the training data, the testing data is used to calculate the different performance metrics. Since, for this experiment, images are resized to two different sizes, we get the following performance metrics for both the image sizes.

Performance Assessment of the CNN Models

As seen in Table 4.2, the features extracted from DenseNet169 performed best for the image sizes of (128, 128, 3) and (256, 256, 3).

TABLE 4.2 Performance Metrics for Approach 2 Image Size (256,256)

MODEL	ACCURACY	PRECISION	RECALL	F1	IMAGE SIZE
Xception	76.76	85.78	69.14	76.566	(128, 128, 3)
VGG16	71.81	73.71	70.64	72.142	(128, 128, 3)
VGG19	78.45	80.61	76.3	78.396	(128, 128, 3)
ResNet50V2	78.84	83.86	74.74	79.038	(128, 128, 3)
ResNet101V2	80.08	83.33	76.82	79.943	(128, 128, 3)
ResNet152V2	80.6	85.58	76.11	80.568	(128, 128, 3)
InceptionV3	69.21	80.96	60.09	68.981	(128, 128, 3)
MobileNet	81.12	86.41	78.65	82.348	(128, 128, 3)
MobileNetV2	81.9	85.45	79.56	82.4	(128, 128, 3)
DenseNet121	72.53	79.1	66.54	72.278	(128, 128, 3)
DenseNet169	**81.77**	**86.23**	**79.1**	**82.511**	**(128, 128, 3)**
DenseNet201	82.68	87.14	78.97	82.854	(128, 128, 3)
Xception	78.32	82.96	74.48	78.492	(256, 256, 3)
VGG16	76.69	78.22	75.52	76.846	(256, 256, 3)
VGG19	83.4	84.76	82.55	83.64	(256, 256, 3)
ResNet50V2	79.04	81.03	77.86	79.413	(256, 256, 3)
ResNet101V2	84.96	85.92	84.24	85.072	(256, 256, 3)
ResNet152V2	82.81	84.22	81.32	82.745	(256, 256, 3)
InceptionV3	61.52	62.81	60.16	61.456	(256, 256, 3)
MobileNet	82.75	84.92	81.05	82.94	(256, 256, 3)
MobileNetV2	81.64	84.24	80.73	82.448	(256, 256, 3)
DenseNet121	81.9	84.99	79.62	82.217	(256, 256, 3)
DenseNet169	**88.02**	**90.14**	**86.91**	**88.496**	**(256, 256, 3)**
DenseNet201	83.85	85.6	82.81	84.182	(256, 256, 3)

The bold signifies the best results in the table.

Summary

In this chapter, we first augmented the images and then performed transfer learning using state of the art CNN models like VGGNet, DenseNet, ResNet, and so on. Python code is provided for DenseNet implementation. Also, experimentation results for other architectures are provided in tables for model performance comparison. In the subsequent chapters, we will perform representation learning by extracting features using these models and then by classifying the extracted features using machine learning models.

Feature Extraction and Representation Learning

5

An end-to-end convolutional neural network comprises two major components. A convolutional layer convolves an image and generates various representations of the image. Once those vector representations are generated, they are fed into a classification layer for the final classification task. The classification layer can be either a machine learning model or a deep neural network model, based on your choice or on the result of your experimentations.

Features can be manually extracted from images by using techniques like SIFT (Wu et al., 2013), SURF (Bay et al., 2006), DAISY (Tola et al., 2010), and so on, or can be manually convolved using known kernels, weights of which are already defined. Further, CNNs can be used to train the network to automatically learn the optimum weights of the kernels used for the convolution process.

STRUCTURE

In this chapter, we will cover the following topics:

- Classification using representation learning
- Treating class imbalance using SMOTE
- Building a classification layer using machine learning algorithms
- Performance assessment of various experimentations

DOI: 10.1201/9781003217381-5

OBJECTIVE

After studying this chapter, you should be able to understand how features are extracted from images using transfer learning, wherein state-of-the-art CNN architectures like Inception (Szegedy et al., 2015), ResNet (He et al., 2016), DenseNet (Huang et al., 2017), and so on will be used. Further, you will also learn how to use the extracted features, which are vector representations of the images to be fed into a classification model for classifying their classes. Lastly, performance metrics for all the experimentations will be created and compared to pick the best performing model.

CLASSIFICATION USING REPRESENTATION LEARNING

Representation learning techniques allow users to extract features from various convolution layers and then ingest those features into a classification model of their choice, whether a machine learning or a deep learning classifier.

In this study, we will experiment with extracting features using various CNN off-the-shelf applications like VGGNet, ResNet, MobileNet, DenseNet, Xception, Inception, and so on, using the representation learning approach and then building RF and SVM classification models to classify among 15 classes (Figure 5.1).

Data Preparation

As a first step for data preparation, the images are converted into numpy arrays. The extracted image arrays will be further used to ingest into convolution layers for feature extraction through the transfer learning technique.

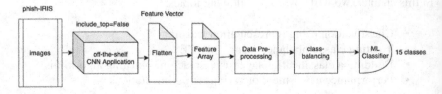

FIGURE 5.1 Classification using representation learning overview.

CONVERT IMAGES TO NUMPY ARRAYS

First we will convert images into numpy arrays. The numpy arrays extracted from train and test data will be saved as numpy array files with the .npy extension for further processing.

OpenCV and numpy libraries in Python are used to convert the images into numpy arrays. Images across training and validation folders are of different sizes. The sizes of the images range from 700 pixels to 1280 pixels in terms of both width and height. Hence, there is a need to resize the images and bring them all to the same size format. Basically, the greater the size of the image, the more pixels are available in the image to extract more low-level features from the images. But by reducing the size of the image, the pixels are contracted and therefore more high-level features will be available to be extracted from the images.

But due to computational limitations we decided to convert the images into arrays of sizes (128, 128, 3) and (256, 256, 3) and find out if the size of the image has any effect on the model performance when extracting relevant features from the image for an effective classification.

For this, we will use the Python OpenCV library.

```
1. import os
2. import glob
3. import cv2
```

Set the data directory and output directory locations. Set the size variable to 512 for resizing the image to a 512×512 array.

```
4. SIZE = 512
5. data_dir="../../../data/phishIRIS/"
6. out_dir=str(SIZE)+"/"
```

Create the train and test data arrays by iterating over the images in each folder within both the train and test dataset folders.

```
7.  # train
8.  train_images = []
9.  train_labels = []
10. for directory_path in glob.glob(data_dir+"train/*"):
11.     train_label = directory_path.split("/")[-1]
12.     for img_path in glob.glob(os.path.
            join(directory_path, "*.*")):
```

```
13.          img = cv2.imread(img_path, cv2.IMREAD_COLOR)
14.          img = cv2.resize(img, (SIZE, SIZE))
15.          img = cv2.cvtColor(img, cv2.COLOR_RGB2BGR)
16.          train_images.append(img)
17.          train_labels.append(train_label)
18.
19. train_images = np.array(train_images)
20. train_labels = np.array(train_labels)
21.
22.
23. # test
24. test_images = []
25. test_labels = []
26. for directory_path in glob.glob(data_dir+"val/*"):
27.     test_label = directory_path.split("/")[-1]
28.     for img_path in glob.glob(os.path.
                     join(directory_path, "*.*")):
29.          img = cv2.imread(img_path, cv2.IMREAD_COLOR)
30.          img = cv2.resize(img, (SIZE, SIZE))
31.          img = cv2.cvtColor(img, cv2.COLOR_RGB2BGR)
32.          test_images.append(img)
33.          test_labels.append(test_label)
34.
35. test_images = np.array(test_images)
36. test_labels = np.array(test_labels)
```

Save the arrays on the disk.

```
37. np.save(out_dir+"train_images", train_images)
38. np.save(out_dir+"test_images", test_images)
39. np.save(out_dir+"train_labels", train_labels)
40. np.save(out_dir+"test_labels", test_labels)
```

Images can be resized to any dimension, and respective numpy arrays can be extracted from images. Images saved on the disk will have the extension of .npy, representing numpy arrays.

Table 5.1 demonstrates the train data and test data dimensions after resizing the images to (128, 128) and (256, 256) height and width dimensions.

There are in total 1313 images in the train folder and 1538 images in the test folder. And since the images are color images, the number of channels is three, representing R(Red), G(Green) and B(Blue) channels.

The train and test label arrays contain the name of the folder in the same sequence as the respective image data is stored in the data array. So, as can be seen in Table 5.1, there are 1313 rows in the train data array, meaning 1313 rows in the train label array, with one label corresponding to each data record.

TABLE 5.1   Training and Testing Data Image Array Dimensions

DATA	DIMENSION (128, 128)	DIMENSION (256, 256)
Train data	(1313, 128, 128, 3)	(1313, 256, 256, 3)
Train labels	(1313,)	(1313,)
Test data	(1539, 128, 128, 3)	(1539, 256, 256, 3)
Test labels	(1539,)	(1539,)

FEATURE EXTRACTION USING CNN OFF-THE-SHELF ARCHITECTURES

In the previous step, raw pixel values are extracted from the images and stored as numpy arrays.

In this step, the raw pixel values of the images will be used to create representations of the images using various off-the-shelf CNN architectures like VGGNet, ResNet, DenseNet, Inception, Exception, and so on.

First, load the required Python libraries.

```
1. import numpy as np
2. import matplotlib.pyplot as plt
3. import glob
4. import cv2
5. import os
6. import seaborn as sns
7. from keras.models import Model, Sequential
8. from keras.layers import Dense, Flatten, Conv2D,
   MaxPooling2D
9. from keras.layers.normalization import
   BatchNormalization
```

Data extracted from the previous step will be used as the input for this step. Hence, set the input and output data directory locations.

```
1. SIZE = 512
2. data_dir="../../data_extractor/"+str(SIZE)+"/"
3. out_dir=str(SIZE)+"/"
4. print(os.listdir(data_dir))
```

```
['train_images.npy', 'test_images.npy', 'test_labels.
npy', 'train_labels.npy']
```

Load the raw pixel value data arrays.

```
1. train_images = np.load(data_dir+'/train_images.npy')
2. test_images = np.load(data_dir+'/test_images.npy')
3. train_labels= np.load(data_dir+'/train_labels.npy')
4. test_labels = np.load(data_dir+'/test_labels.npy')
```

The labels are in a raw text format; hence they need to encode the labels from text to integers using the sklearn LabelEncoder module.

```
1. from sklearn import preprocessing
2. le = preprocessing.LabelEncoder()
3. le.fit(train_labels)
4. train_labels_encoded = le.transform(train_labels)
5. test_labels_encoded = le.transform(test_labels)
```

Pickle the label encoder for future inverse encoding of labels to text for plotting a confusion matrix and classification reports.

```
6. #pickle the label encoder
7. np.save(out_dir+'label_encoder.npy', le.classes_)
```

Rename the datasets to standard naming conventions used for machine learning processing.

```
1. x_train, y_train, x_test, y_test = train_images,
   train_labels_encoded, test_images, test_labels_encoded
```

Normalize the pixel values to bring them between 0 and 1.

```
1. x_train, x_test = x_train / 255.0, x_test / 255.0
```

Save the train and test labels to disk.

```
1. np.save(out_dir+"train_labels", y_train)
2. np.save(out_dir+"test_labels", y_test)
```

Next, we will extract features using various off-the-shelf CNN architectures.

XCEPTION

```
1. from keras.applications.xception import Xception
2.
```

```
3.  # Load model without classifier/fully connected
    layers
4.  model = Xception(weights='imagenet', include_
    top=False, input_shape=(SIZE, SIZE, 3))
5.
6.  # Make loaded layers as non-trainable because we
    want to work with pre-trained weights
7.  for layer in model.layers:
8.      layer.trainable = False
9.
10. model.summary()
11.
12. # Send train data from feature extractor process
13. feature_extractor=model.predict(x_train)
14. features = feature_extractor.reshape(feature_
    extractor.shape[0], -1)
15.
16. # Send test data through same feature extractor
    process
17. X_test_feature = model.predict(x_test)
18. X_test_features = X_test_feature.reshape(X_test_
    feature.shape[0], -1)
19.
20. np.save(out_dir+"Xception_train_images", features)
21. np.save(out_dir+"Xception_test_images",
    X_test_features)
```

On observing the last few layers of the Xception model and parameter details, trainable parameters are 0, since we are using pre-trained weights from the Xception module, which was trained on an imagenet dataset.

```
block14_sepconv1 (SeparableConv (None, 16, 16, 1536) 1582080     add_11[0][0]
_____
block14_sepconv1_bn (BatchNorma (None, 16, 16, 1536) 6144        block14_sepconv1[0][0]
_____
block14_sepconv1_act (Activatio (None, 16, 16, 1536) 0           block14_sepconv1_bn[0][0]
_____
block14_sepconv2 (SeparableConv (None, 16, 16, 2048) 3159552     block14_sepconv1_act[0][0]
_____
block14_sepconv2_bn (BatchNorma (None, 16, 16, 2048) 8192        block14_sepconv2[0][0]
_____
block14_sepconv2_act (Activatio (None, 16, 16, 2048) 0           block14_sepconv2_bn[0][0]
================================================================================
Total params: 20,861,480
Trainable params: 0
Non-trainable params: 20,861,480
```

VGG19

```
1.  from keras.applications.vgg19 import VGG19
2.
3.  model = VGG19(weights='imagenet', include_top=False,
    input_shape=(SIZE, SIZE, 3))
4.
5.  for layer in model.layers:
6.      layer.trainable = False
7.
8.  print(model.summary())
9.
10. feature_extractor=model.predict(x_train)
11. features = feature_extractor.reshape(feature_
    extractor.shape[0], -1)
12.
13. X_test_feature = model.predict(x_test)
14. X_test_features = X_test_feature.reshape(X_test_
    feature.shape[0], -1)
15.
16. np.save(out_dir+"VGG19_train_images", features)
17. np.save(out_dir+"VGG19_test_images",
    X_test_features)
```

Model: "vgg19"

Layer (type)	Output Shape	Param #
input_3 (InputLayer)	[(None, 512, 512, 3)]	0
block1_conv1 (Conv2D)	(None, 512, 512, 64)	1792
block1_conv2 (Conv2D)	(None, 512, 512, 64)	36928
block1_pool (MaxPooling2D)	(None, 256, 256, 64)	0
block2_conv1 (Conv2D)	(None, 256, 256, 128)	73856
block2_conv2 (Conv2D)	(None, 256, 256, 128)	147584
block2_pool (MaxPooling2D)	(None, 128, 128, 128)	0
block3_conv1 (Conv2D)	(None, 128, 128, 256)	295168
block3_conv2 (Conv2D)	(None, 128, 128, 256)	590080
block3_conv3 (Conv2D)	(None, 128, 128, 256)	590080
block3_conv4 (Conv2D)	(None, 128, 128, 256)	590080
block3_pool (MaxPooling2D)	(None, 64, 64, 256)	0
block4_conv1 (Conv2D)	(None, 64, 64, 512)	1180160
block4_conv2 (Conv2D)	(None, 64, 64, 512)	2359808
block4_conv3 (Conv2D)	(None, 64, 64, 512)	2359808
block4_conv4 (Conv2D)	(None, 64, 64, 512)	2359808
block4_pool (MaxPooling2D)	(None, 32, 32, 512)	0
block5_conv1 (Conv2D)	(None, 32, 32, 512)	2359808
block5_conv2 (Conv2D)	(None, 32, 32, 512)	2359808
block5_conv3 (Conv2D)	(None, 32, 32, 512)	2359808
block5_conv4 (Conv2D)	(None, 32, 32, 512)	2359808
block5_pool (MaxPooling2D)	(None, 16, 16, 512)	0

Total params: 20,024,384
Trainable params: 0
Non-trainable params: 20,024,384

RESNET50

```
1.  from keras.applications.resnet50 import ResNet50
2.
3.  model = ResNet50(weights='imagenet', include_
    top=False, input_shape=(SIZE, SIZE, 3))
4.
5.  for layer in model.layers:
6.      layer.trainable = False
7.
8.  print(model.summary())
9.
10. feature_extractor=model.predict(x_train)
11. features = feature_extractor.reshape(feature_
    extractor.shape[0], -1)
12.
13. X_test_feature = model.predict(x_test)
14. X_test_features = X_test_feature.reshape(X_test_
    feature.shape[0], -1)
15.
16. np.save(out_dir+"ResNet50_train_images", features)
17. np.save(out_dir+"ResNet50_test_images",
    X_test_features)
```

Last few layers and parameter details of ResNet50 model.

conv5_block2_out (Activation)	(None, 16, 16, 2048)	0	conv5_block2_add[0][0]
conv5_block3_1_conv (Conv2D)	(None, 16, 16, 512)	1049088	conv5_block2_out[0][0]
conv5_block3_1_bn (BatchNormali	(None, 16, 16, 512)	2048	conv5_block3_1_conv[0][0]
conv5_block3_1_relu (Activation	(None, 16, 16, 512)	0	conv5_block3_1_bn[0][0]
conv5_block3_2_conv (Conv2D)	(None, 16, 16, 512)	2359808	conv5_block3_1_relu[0][0]
conv5_block3_2_bn (BatchNormali	(None, 16, 16, 512)	2048	conv5_block3_2_conv[0][0]
conv5_block3_2_relu (Activation	(None, 16, 16, 512)	0	conv5_block3_2_bn[0][0]
conv5_block3_3_conv (Conv2D)	(None, 16, 16, 2048)	1050624	conv5_block3_2_relu[0][0]
conv5_block3_3_bn (BatchNormali	(None, 16, 16, 2048)	8192	conv5_block3_3_conv[0][0]
conv5_block3_add (Add)	(None, 16, 16, 2048)	0	conv5_block2_out[0][0] conv5_block3_3_bn[0][0]
conv5_block3_out (Activation)	(None, 16, 16, 2048)	0	conv5_block3_add[0][0]

```
==================================================
Total params: 23,587,712
Trainable params: 0
Non-trainable params: 23,587,712
```

We followed a similar process to extract features using ResNet101, ResNet152, ResNet50V2, RestNet101V2 and ResNet152V2.

INCEPTIONV3

```
1.  from keras.applications.inception_v3 import
    InceptionV3
2.
3.  model = InceptionV3(weights='imagenet', include_
    top=False, input_shape=(SIZE, SIZE, 3))
4.
5.  for layer in model.layers:
6.      layer.trainable = False
7.
8.  print(model.summary())
9.
10. feature_extractor=model.predict(x_train)
11. features = feature_extractor.reshape(feature_
    extractor.shape[0], -1)
12.
13. X_test_feature = model.predict(x_test)
14. X_test_features = X_test_feature.reshape(X_test_
    feature.shape[0], -1)
15.
16. np.save(out_dir+"InceptionV3_train_images",
    features)
17. np.save(out_dir+"InceptionV3_test_images",
    X_test_features)
```

INCEPTIONRESNETV2

```
1.  from keras.applications.inception_resnet_v2 import
    InceptionResNetV2
2.
3.  model = InceptionResNetV2(weights='imagenet',
    include_top=False, input_shape=(SIZE, SIZE, 3))
4.
```

```
5.  for layer in model.layers:
6.      layer.trainable = False
7.
8.  print(model.summary())
9.
10. feature_extractor=model.predict(x_train)
11. features = feature_extractor.reshape(feature_
    extractor.shape[0], -1)
12.
13. X_test_feature = model.predict(x_test)
14. X_test_features = X_test_feature.reshape(X_test_
    feature.shape[0], -1)
15.
16. np.save(out_dir+"InceptionResNetV2_train_images",
    features)
17. np.save(out_dir+"InceptionResNetV2_test_images",
    X_test_features)
```

MOBILENET

```
1.  from keras.applications.mobilenet import MobileNet
2.
3.  model = MobileNet(weights='imagenet', include_
    top=False, input_shape=(SIZE, SIZE, 3))
4.
5.  for layer in model.layers:
6.      layer.trainable = False
7.
8.  print(model.summary())
9.
10. feature_extractor=model.predict(x_train)
11. features = feature_extractor.reshape(feature_
    extractor.shape[0], -1)
12.
13. X_test_feature = model.predict(x_test)
14. X_test_features = X_test_feature.reshape(X_test_
    feature.shape[0], -1)
15.
16. np.save(out_dir+"MobileNet_train_images", features)
17. np.save(out_dir+"MobileNet_test_images",
    X_test_features)
```

We followed the same process to extract features from the MobileNetV2 architecture.

DENSENET121

```
1.  from keras.applications.densenet import DenseNet121
2.
3.  model = DenseNet121(weights='imagenet', include_
    top=False, input_shape=(SIZE, SIZE, 3))
4.
5.  for layer in model.layers:
6.      layer.trainable = False
7.
8.  print(model.summary())
9.
10. feature_extractor=model.predict(x_train)
11. features = feature_extractor.reshape(feature_
    extractor.shape[0], -1)
12.
13. X_test_feature = model.predict(x_test)
14. X_test_features = X_test_feature.reshape(X_test_
    feature.shape[0], -1)
15.
16. np.save(out_dir+"DenseNet121_train_images",
    features)
17. np.save(out_dir+"DenseNet121_test_images",
    X_test_features)
```

We followed the same process to extract features from the DenseNet169 and DenseNet201 architectures.

Finally, all the features are extracted using various CNN architectures using the raw pixel values extracted from the images by resizing the images to 128×128, 256×256 and 512×512, and are saved to the disk (see Figure 5.2).

Table 5.2 demonstrates the training and testing data feature dimensions after extracting features using various CNN applications.

Handling Class Imbalance

Class imbalance is a situation wherein data in each class are non-uniformly distributed in the dataset for training the model. This may result in the model skewing toward the class which has the maximum number of records available

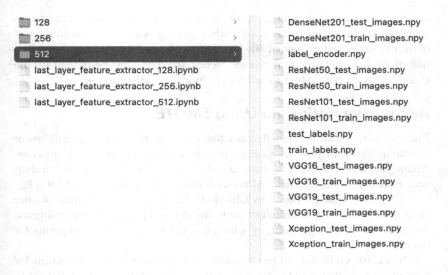

FIGURE 5.2   Disk arrangement of image features arrays.

TABLE 5.2   Extracted Feature Dimensions of the Training and Testing Dataset

| | TRAINING IMAGE SIZE | | TESTING IMAGE SIZE | |
APPLICATION	(128, 128, 3)	(256, 256, 3)	(128, 128, 3)	(256, 256, 3)
Xception	(1313, 32768)	(1313, 131072)	(1539, 32768)	(1539, 131072)
VGG16	(1313, 8192)	(1313, 32768)	(1539, 8192)	(1539, 32768)
VGG19	(1313, 8192)	(1313, 32768)	(1539, 8192)	(1539, 32768)
s	(1313, 32768)	(1313, 131072)	(1539, 32768)	(1539, 131072)
ResNet101V2	(1313, 32768)	(1313, 131072)	(1539, 32768)	(1539, 131072)
ResNet152V2	(1313, 32768)	(1313, 131072)	(1539, 32768)	(1539, 131072)
InceptionV3	(1313, 8192)	(1313, 73728)	(1539, 8192)	(1539, 73728)
InceptionResNetV2	(1313, 6144)	(1313, 55296)	(1539, 6144)	(1539, 55296)
MobileNet	(1313, 16384)	(1313, 65536)	(1539, 16384)	(1539, 65536)
MobileNetV2	(1313, 20480)	(1313, 81920)	(1539, 20480)	(1539, 81920)
DenseNet121	(1313, 16384)	(1313, 65536)	(1539, 16384)	(1539, 65536)
DenseNet169	(1313, 26624)	(1313, 106496)	(1539, 26624)	(1539, 106496)
DenseNet201	(1313, 30720)	(1313, 122880)	(1539, 30720)	(1539, 122880)

for the training, as the model has more records available to learn from that one particular class. Hence, features from that particular class take precedence in the learning of the model. This results in various anomalies in the model training process, and hence data must be pre-processed and handled for the class imbalance before ingesting it into the model training process.

For a Phish-IRIS dataset, as can be seen in Table 3.1, the number of images available for the "other" class is 400, whereas images available for all the rest of the classes is in the range of 50–150. This is clearly an imbalanced distribution of the data in individual classes. Hence, the data must be treated for the class imbalance before being used for the model training purpose.

Adding Synthetic Data Using SMOTE

The imbalanced dataset is handled by either undersampling the majority class or oversampling the majority class. Both approaches have their own pros and cons. Among the more advanced techniques which are widely used for class imbalance treatment is the Synthetic Minority Over-sampling Technique (SMOTE).

This technique, proposed by Chawla et al. (2002), works by first placing all the data points of the dataset in the n-dimensional plane, and then using the K-nearest neighbor algorithm, by which it generates synthetic data points for the minority class.

Since, for a multi-class classification, the maximum number of records for a given class, in this case the "other" class, is 400, synthetic data will need to be added to all the other classes to make their numbers 400. Since there are 15 classes in total, after applying the oversampling technique of SMOTE the total number of records in each class will become 400, making the total number of training data 6000, that is 400×15.

Table 5.3 demonstrates the training data array dimensions after applying SMOTE for various CNN applications.

TABLE 5.3   Training Data Dimensions after Applying SMOTE

APPLICATION	IMAGE SIZE (128, 128, 3)	IMAGE SIZE (256, 256, 3)
Xception	(6000, 32768)	(6000, 131072)
VGG16	(6000, 8192)	(6000, 32768)
VGG19	(6000, 8192)	(6000, 32768)
ResNet50V2	(6000, 32768)	(6000, 131072)
ResNet101V2	(6000, 32768)	(6000, 131072)
ResNet152V2	(6000, 32768)	(6000, 131072)
InceptionV3	(6000, 8192)	(6000, 73728)
InceptionResNetV2	(6000, 6144)	(6000, 55296)
MobileNet	(6000, 16384)	(6000, 65536)
MobileNetV2	(6000, 20480)	(6000, 81920)
DenseNet121	(6000, 16384)	(6000, 65536)
DenseNet169	(6000, 26624)	(6000, 106496)
DenseNet201	(6000, 30720)	(6000, 122880)

SMOTE PYTHON IMPLEMENTATION

Input data will be the features extracted in the previous stage using various CNN architectures.

```
1. SIZE=512
2. data_dir="../feature_extractor/
   last_layer/"+str(SIZE)+"/"
3. out_dir="last_layer/"+str(SIZE)+"/"
```

We will create a Python list with all the CNN architectures to extract the image features.

```
1.  list_of_architectures = [
2.      "Xception",
3.      "VGG16",
4.      "VGG19",
5.      "ResNet50",
6.      "ResNet101",
7.      "ResNet152",
8.      "ResNet50V2",
9.      "ResNet101V2",
10.     "ResNet152V2",
11.     "InceptionV3",
12.     "InceptionResNetV2",
13.     "MobileNet",
14.     "MobileNetV2",
15.     "DenseNet121",
16.     "DenseNet169",
17.     "DenseNet201"
18.
19. ]
```

The below function will load the features extracted by the respective CNN architecture, and then will apply the SMOTE algorithm to produce synthetic data points for the classes that are less in number with respect to other dominant classes in the dataset.

For example, the "other" class has 400 images, and that is the most dominant number of images for a particular class in the dataset. So, synthetic images will be created for all other classes so that the final number of images for each class will become 400. So, the "PayPal" class has 121 images, hence 279 synthetic images will be generated for the "PayPal" class. And the same will be followed for all other classes.

```
1. def getSMOTE(model):
2.     X_SMOTE = np.load(data_dir+model+"_train_images.npy")
3.     y_train = np.load(data_dir+'/train_labels.npy')
4.
5.     # SMOTE
6.     from imblearn.over_sampling import SMOTE
7.     oversample = SMOTE()
8.     X_train_SMOTE, y_train_SMOTE = oversample.fit_
       resample(X_SMOTE, y_train)
9.
10.    np.save(out_dir+model+"_X_train_SMOTE", X_train_SMOTE)
11.    np.save(out_dir+model+"_y_train_SMOTE",
       y_train_SMOTE)
```

Now, the above function is called iteratively for all the CNN architectures using the list which is created before.

```
1. for arch in list_of_architectures:
2.     getSMOTE(arch)
```

At the end of the loop, all the features extracted using various CNN architectures will have an augmented number of datapoints.

MACHINE LEARNING CLASSIFIER

Features extracted from all the CNN architectures are then ingested into the machine learning classifiers as a multi-class classification problem.

Create a list of all CNN architectures for which we have extracted features and want to build a classifier.

```
1. list_of_architectures = [
2.     "Xception",
3.     "VGG16",
4.     "VGG19",
5.     "ResNet50",
6.     "ResNet101",
7.     "ResNet152",
8.     "ResNet50V2",
9.     "ResNet101V2",
10.    "ResNet152V2",
11.    "InceptionV3",
```

```
12.      "InceptionResNetV2",
13.      "MobileNet",
14.      "MobileNetV2",
15.      "DenseNet121",
16.      "DenseNet169",
17.      "DenseNet201"
18.
19.]
```

Create a list of machine learning algorithms that we will use to build a classifier.

```
1. list_of_classifiers = [
2.      "RF",
3.      "SVM"
4.]
```

Create a list of sizes for which images are resized and features extracted.

```
1. list_of_size = [
2.      128,
3.      256,
4.      512
5.]
```

Set some variables.

```
1. layer = "last_layer"
2. preprocessing_technique = "smote"
```

Create a reusable data reading function.

```
1. def getData(model, image_size):
2.      train_data_dir="../class_imabalance/" + layer +
         "/" + str(image_size)+"/"
3.      test_data_dir="../feature_extractor/" + layer +
         "/" + str(image_size)+"/"
4.      X_train=np.load(train_data_dir+model+"_X_train_
         SMOTE.npy")
5.      y_train=np.load(train_data_dir+model+"_y_train_
         SMOTE.npy")
6.      X_test=np.load(test_data_dir+model+"_test_images.
         npy")
7.      y_test=np.load(test_data_dir+"test_labels.npy")
8.      return X_train, y_train, X_test, y_test
```

Create a reusable label encoder reader function.

```
1. def getLabelEncoder(layer, image_size):
2.     label_encoder_location = "../feature_extractor/"
       + layer + "/" + str(image_size)+"/"
3.     label_encoder = np.load(label_encoder_
       location+'label_encoder.npy')
4.     return label_encoder
```

Create a reusable function.

```
1. def getClassificationMetrics(test_labels,
   prediction):
2.     from sklearn.metrics import confusion_matrix
3.     test_label_list=list(np.unique(test_labels))
4.     cnf_matrix = confusion_matrix(test_labels,
       prediction,labels=test_label_list)
5.     np.set_printoptions(precision=2)
6.
7.     # Plot non-normalized confusion matrix
8.     plt.figure(figsize=(8,8))
9.     plot_confusion_matrix(cnf_matrix,
       classes=test_label_list,
10.    title='Confusion matrix, without normalization')
11.
12.
13.    from sklearn import metrics
14.
15.    accuracy = round(metrics.accuracy_score(test_
       labels, prediction),3)
16.    precision = round(metrics.precision_score(test_
       labels, prediction, average='weighted'),3)
17.    recall = round(metrics.recall_score(test_labels,
       prediction, average='weighted'),3)
18.    f1_score = round(metrics.f1_score(test_labels,
       prediction, average='weighted'),3)
19.
20.
21.    FP = cnf_matrix.sum(axis=0) - np.diag(cnf_matrix)
22.    FN = cnf_matrix.sum(axis=1) - np.diag(cnf_matrix)
23.    TP = np.diag(cnf_matrix)
24.    TN = cnf_matrix.sum() - (FP + FN + TP)
25.
26.    # Sensitivity, hit rate, recall, or true positive
       rate
27.    TPR = round((TP/(TP+FN)).mean(),3)
```

```
28.    # Specificity or true negative rate
29.    TNR = round((TN/(TN+FP) ).mean(),3)
30.    # Precision or positive predictive value
31.    PPV = round((TP/(TP+FP)).mean(),3)
32.    # Negative predictive value
33.    NPV = round((TN/(TN+FN)).mean(),3)
34.    # Fall out or false positive rate
35.    FPR = round((FP/(FP+TN)).mean(),3)
36.    # False negative rate
37.    FNR = round((FN/(TP+FN)).mean(),3)
38.    # False discovery rate
39.    FDR = round((FP/(TP+FP)).mean(),3)
40.
41.    # Balanced metrics
42.    balanced_accuracy = round(metrics.balanced_
       accuracy_score(test_labels, prediction),3)
43.    balanced_precision = PPV
44.    balanced_recall = TPR
45.    balanced_f1 = round((2*(PPV*TPR)/(PPV+TPR)),3)
46.
47.    print("Acc= ", accuracy)
48.    print("Pre= ", precision)
49.    print("Rec= ", recall)
50.    print("F1= ", f1_score)
51.    print("")
52.
53.    print("Bal_Acc = ", balanced_accuracy)
54.    print("Bal_Pre = ", balanced_precision)
55.    print("Bal_Rec = ", balanced_recall)
56.    print("Bal_F1= ", balanced_f1)
57.    print("")
58.
59.    from sklearn.metrics import classification_
       report, confusion_matrix
60.    print(classification_report(test_labels,
       prediction))
61.
62.    return accuracy, precision, recall, f1_score,
       balanced_accuracy, balanced_precision, balanced_
       recall, balanced_f1
```

Create a reusable function.

```
1. def classify(model_name, classifier, image_size):
2.     X_train, y_train, X_test, y_test =
       getData(model_name, image_size)
```

```
3.
4.     if classifier == "RF":
5.         from sklearn.ensemble import RandomForestClassifier
6.         model = RandomForestClassifier(n_estimators =
           100, random_state = 42)
7.     elif classifier == "SVM":
8.         from sklearn.svm import SVC
9.         model = SVC(kernel='linear', degree=3, C=1,
           decision_function_shape='ovo')
10.
11.    # Train the model on training data
12.    model.fit(X_train, y_train) #For sklearn no one
       hot encoding
13.
14.    #Now predict using the trained RF model.
15.    prediction = model.predict(X_test)
16.
17.    #get the encoder from the pickle file
18.    from sklearn import preprocessing
19.    le = preprocessing.LabelEncoder()
20.    le.classes_ = getLabelEncoder(layer, image_size)
21.
22.    #Inverse le transform to get original label back.
23.    prediction = le.inverse_transform(prediction)
24.    y_test = le.inverse_transform(y_test)
25.
26.    accuracy, precision, recall, f1_score, balanced_
       accuracy, balanced_precision, balanced_recall,
       balanced_f1 = getClassificationMetrics(y_test,
       prediction)
27.    return accuracy, precision, recall, f1_score,
       balanced_accuracy, balanced_precision, balanced_
       recall, balanced_f1
```

Finally, run the loop.

```
1. list_of_analysis=[]
2. for image_size in list_of_size:
3.     for classifier in list_of_classifiers:
4.         for model in list_of_architectures:
5.             print("------------------------------------
               ----------------------------------------")
6.             print(classifier + " - " + model + " - " +
               str(image_size))
```

```
7.      print("")
8.      accuracy, precision, recall, f1_score,
        balanced_accuracy, balanced_precision,
        balanced_recall, balanced_f1 =
        classify(model, classifier, image_size)
9.      list_of_analysis.append(
10.        [
11.          classifier, model, image_size, accuracy,
             precision, recall, f1_score, balanced_
             accuracy, balanced_precision, balanced_
             recall, balanced_f1
12.        ]
13.      )
```

PERFORMANCE ASSESSMENT OF VARIOUS EXPERIMENTATIONS

As can be seen from the performance metrics in Table 5.4, using the representation learning approach for multi-class classification, the VGG16, MobileNet and DenseNet201 applications performed best for different image sizes. DenseNet201 performed exceptionally well for the image size of (256, 256, 3) using the SVM classifier, with accuracy, precision, recall and f1 score exceeding 90%.

Summary

In this chapter, we extracted pixel values from images as a numpy array. Then, with those pixel values ingested into state-of-the-art CNN models, features are extracted using various CNN models. Then imbalance class treatment is performed on the extracted feature dataset. Further, those features were used to train Random Forest and Support Vector Machine classification models. In the subsequent chapter, we will perform dimensionality reduction of the features extracted using CNN models in this chapter and will then use the extracted features to train the RF and SVM classification models.

TABLE 5.4 Performance Metrics for Multi-Class Classification Using RF and SVM

MODEL	ACCURACY	PRECISION	RECALL	F1_SCORE	FPR	IMAGE SIZE	CLASSIFIER
Xception	0.802	0.81	0.802	0.802	0.021	(128, 128, 3)	Random Forest
VGG16	**0.885**	**0.887**	**0.885**	**0.88**	**0.015**	(128, 128, 3)	Random Forest
VGG19	0.862	0.862	0.862	0.858	0.017	(128, 128, 3)	Random Forest
ResNet50V2	0.851	0.853	0.851	0.842	0.021	(128, 128, 3)	Random Forest
ResNet101V2	0.841	0.847	0.841	0.835	0.022	(128, 128, 3)	Random Forest
ResNet152V2	0.838	0.845	0.838	0.831	0.022	(128, 128, 3)	Random Forest
InceptionV3	0.788	0.799	0.788	0.787	0.024	(128, 128, 3)	Random Forest
InceptionResNetV2	0.801	0.811	0.801	0.8	0.022	(128, 128, 3)	Random Forest
MobileNet	0.867	0.868	0.867	0.858	0.019	(128, 128, 3)	Random Forest
MobileNetV2	0.869	0.87	0.869	0.861	0.019	(128, 128, 3)	Random Forest
DenseNet121	0.867	0.869	0.867	0.863	0.017	(128, 128, 3)	Random Forest
DenseNet169	0.878	0.877	0.878	0.874	0.015	(128, 128, 3)	Random Forest
DenseNet201	0.88	0.878	0.88	0.875	0.016	(128, 128, 3)	Random Forest
Xception	0.791	0.818	0.791	0.798	0.02	(128, 128, 3)	SVM
VGG16	0.836	0.857	0.836	0.841	0.015	(128, 128, 3)	SVM
VGG19	0.809	0.838	0.809	0.817	0.018	(128, 128, 3)	SVM
ResNet50V2	0.84	0.852	0.84	0.842	0.016	(128, 128, 3)	SVM
ResNet101V2	0.834	0.843	0.834	0.835	0.018	(128, 128, 3)	SVM
ResNet152V2	0.832	0.847	0.832	0.834	0.018	(128, 128, 3)	SVM
InceptionV3	0.769	0.799	0.769	0.777	0.022	(128, 128, 3)	SVM
InceptionResNetV2	0.815	0.83	0.815	0.818	0.019	(128, 128, 3)	SVM

(Continued)

TABLE 5.4 (CONTINUED) Performance Metrics for Multi-Class Classification Using RF and SVM

MODEL	ACCURACY	PRECISION	RECALL	F1_SCORE	FPR	IMAGE SIZE	CLASSIFIER
MobileNet	**0.891**	**0.894**	**0.891**	**0.89**	**0.012**	(128, 128, 3)	SVM
MobileNetV2	0.871	0.879	0.871	0.87	0.014	(128, 128, 3)	SVM
DenseNet121	0.817	0.841	0.817	0.823	0.017	(128, 128, 3)	SVM
DenseNet169	0.841	0.859	0.841	0.846	0.015	(128, 128, 3)	SVM
DenseNet201	0.856	0.863	0.856	0.857	0.015	(128, 128, 3)	SVM
Xception	0.836	0.84	0.836	0.833	0.021	(256, 256, 3)	Random Forest
VGG16	0.886	0.889	0.886	0.88	0.017	(256, 256, 3)	Random Forest
VGG19	0.884	0.887	0.884	0.878	0.017	(256, 256, 3)	Random Forest
ResNet50V2	0.864	0.868	0.864	0.851	0.022	(256, 256, 3)	Random Forest
ResNet101V2	0.863	0.866	0.863	0.851	0.022	(256, 256, 3)	Random Forest
ResNet152V2	0.86	0.868	0.86	0.847	0.025	(256, 256, 3)	Random Forest
InceptionV3	0.812	0.825	0.812	0.804	0.026	(256, 256, 3)	Random Forest
InceptionResNetV2	0.83	0.835	0.83	0.823	0.022	(256, 256, 3)	Random Forest
MobileNet	0.86	0.868	0.86	0.849	0.023	(256, 256, 3)	Random Forest
MobileNetV2	0.865	0.865	0.865	0.854	0.021	(256, 256, 3)	Random Forest
DenseNet121	0.888	0.888	0.888	0.882	0.016	(256, 256, 3)	Random Forest
DenseNet169	0.886	0.885	0.886	0.88	0.017	(256, 256, 3)	Random Forest
DenseNet201	**0.897**	**0.897**	**0.897**	**0.89**	**0.016**	(256, 256, 3)	Random Forest
Xception	0.84	0.85	0.84	0.842	0.016	(256, 256, 3)	SVM
VGG16	0.886	0.888	0.886	0.885	0.013	(256, 256, 3)	SVM
VGG19	0.876	0.877	0.876	0.875	0.015	(256, 256, 3)	SVM

(Continued)

TABLE 5.4 (CONTINUED) Performance Metrics for Multi-Class Classification Using RF and SVM

MODEL	ACCURACY	PRECISION	RECALL	F1_SCORE	FPR	IMAGE SIZE	CLASSIFIER
ResNet50V2	0.863	0.87	0.863	0.862	0.015	(256, 256, 3)	SVM
ResNet101V2	0.853	0.864	0.853	0.854	0.016	(256, 256, 3)	SVM
ResNet152V2	0.879	0.883	0.879	0.878	0.014	(256, 256, 3)	SVM
InceptionV3	0.877	0.879	0.877	0.874	0.015	(256, 256, 3)	SVM
InceptionResNetV2	0.846	0.858	0.846	0.846	0.017	(256, 256, 3)	SVM
MobileNet	0.897	0.897	0.897	0.893	0.014	(256, 256, 3)	SVM
MobileNetV2	0.891	0.892	0.891	0.889	0.013	(256, 256, 3)	SVM
DenseNet121	0.878	0.882	0.878	0.878	0.014	(256, 256, 3)	SVM
DenseNet169	0.897	0.899	0.897	0.896	0.012	(256, 256, 3)	SVM
DenseNet201	**0.903**	**0.906**	**0.903**	**0.903**	**0.011**	(256, 256, 3)	SVM

The bold signifies the best results in the table.

Dimensionality Reduction Techniques

6

Principal Component Analysis (PCA) is the most prevalent dimensionality reduction technique. Any point in an n-dimensional space can be represented in a lower-dimensional plane using PCA. The advantages of reducing dimensions of the data points are many. Some of the important advantages of data compression are lower storage requirements, reduced computational time and cost and eliminating redundant features. Once features are extracted from images, the dimensions of those image vector representations can be reduced using PCA before feeding them into a classification layer.

STRUCTURE

In this chapter, we will cover the following topics:

- Basics of dimensionality reduction
- PCA implementation using Python
- Performance assessment of various experimentations

OBJECTIVE

After studying this chapter, you should be aware of how the dimensionality reduction technique can be quickly implemented on data points using PCA and its implementation in Python.

DOI: 10.1201/9781003217381-6

DIMENSIONALITY REDUCTION USING PCA

We will also experiment with dimensionality reduction of the feature vectors extracted in the previous sections and retrain the classification model to validate if reducing the dimensions of the extracted features improves the result (Figure 6.1).

PCA Python Implementation

```
1. from sklearn.decomposition import IncrementalPCA
2. pca = IncrementalPCA(n_components=n_components)
3. X_train = pca.fit_transform(X_train)
4. X_test = pca.transform(X_test)
```

Before X_train and X_test are ingested in the model for training and testing, respectively, they are PCA'd using the Python PCA implementation. Hence, for the classification process to remain intact, just the X_train and X_test data are transformed from their original features to PCA'd features.

Basically, even if the data dimensions are different when the features are extracted using various CNN applications, after PCA treatment, all the data are converted to the same dimensions. Table 6.1 demonstrates the dimensions of the training data after their dimensions are reduced to 50, 100 and 500 using the PCA technique.

Import required libraries.

```
1.  import glob
2.  import cv2
3.  import os
4.  import numpy as np
5.  import matplotlib.pyplot as plt
6.  import seaborn as sns
7.
8.  from keras.models import Model, Sequential
9.  from keras.layers import Dense, Flatten, Conv2D,
    MaxPooling2D
10. from keras.layers.normalization import
    BatchNormalization
```

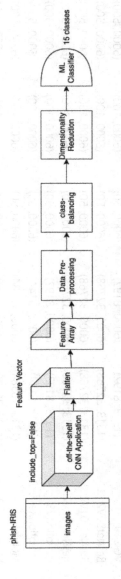

FIGURE 6.1   Classification using dimensionality reduction overview.

TABLE 6.1 Training Data Dimensions after Reducing Dimensions Using PCA

APPLICATION	IMAGE SIZE (128, 128, 3)	SMOTE DATA	PCA WITH 50 DIMENSIONS	PCA WITH 100 DIMENSIONS	PCA WITH 500 DIMENSIONS
Xception	(1313, 32768)	(6000, 32768)	(6000, 50)	(6000, 100)	(6000, 500)
VGG16	(1313, 8192)	(6000, 8192)	(6000, 50)	(6000, 100)	(6000, 500)
VGG19	(1313, 8192)	(6000, 8192)	(6000, 50)	(6000, 100)	(6000, 500)
ResNet50V2	(1313, 32768)	(6000, 32768)	(6000, 50)	(6000, 100)	(6000, 500)
ResNet101V2	(1313, 32768)	(6000, 32768)	(6000, 50)	(6000, 100)	(6000, 500)
ResNet152V2	(1313, 32768)	(6000, 32768)	(6000, 50)	(6000, 100)	(6000, 500)
InceptionV3	(1313, 8192)	(6000, 8192)	(6000, 50)	(6000, 100)	(6000, 500)
InceptionResNetV2	(1313, 6144)	(6000, 6144)	(6000, 50)	(6000, 100)	(6000, 500)
MobileNet	(1313, 16384)	(6000, 16384)	(6000, 50)	(6000, 100)	(6000, 500)
MobileNetV2	(1313, 20480)	(6000, 20480)	(6000, 50)	(6000, 100)	(6000, 500)
DenseNet121	(1313, 16384)	(6000, 16384)	(6000, 50)	(6000, 100)	(6000, 500)
DenseNet169	(1313, 26624)	(6000, 26624)	(6000, 50)	(6000, 100)	(6000, 500)
DenseNet201	(1313, 30720)	(6000, 30720)	(6000, 50)	(6000, 100)	(6000, 500)

Create the list of all CNN architectures.

```
1.  list_of_architectures = [
2.      "Xception",
3.      "VGG16",
4.      "VGG19",
5.      "ResNet50",
6.      "ResNet101",
7.      "ResNet152",
8.      "ResNet50V2",
9.      "ResNet101V2",
10.     "ResNet152V2",
11.     "InceptionV3",
12.     "InceptionResNetV2",
13.     "MobileNet",
14.     "MobileNetV2",
15.     "DenseNet121",
16.     "DenseNet169",
17.     "DenseNet201"
18.
19. ]
```

Create the list of classifiers.

```
1.  list_of_classifiers = [
2.      "RF",
3.      "SVM"
4.  ]
```

Create the list of image sizes from which features are extracted.

```
1.  list_of_size = [
2.      128,
3.      256
4.  ]
```

Reusable function to read the data from the disk.

```
1.  def getData(model, image_size, n_components):
2.      X_data_dir="../pca/" + layer + "/" +
        str(image_size)+"/"
3.      y_train_data_dir="../class_imabalance/" + layer +
        "/" + str(image_size)+"/"
4.      y_test_data_dir="../feature_extractor/" + layer +
        "/" + str(image_size)+"/"
```

```
5.    X_train=np.load(X_data_dir+model+"_train_" +
      str(n_components) + ".npy")
6.    y_train=np.load(y_train_data_dir+model+"_y_
      train_SMOTE.npy")
7.    X_test=np.load(X_data_dir+model+"_test_" +
      str(n_components) + ".npy")
8.    y_test=np.load(y_test_data_dir+"test_labels.npy")
9.    return X_train, y_train, X_test, y_test
```

Reusable function for reading the label encoder from the disk.

```
1. def getLabelEncoder(layer, image_size):
2.    label_encoder_location = "../feature_extractor/"
      + layer + "/" + str(image_size)+"/"
3.    label_encoder = np.load(label_encoder_
      location+'label_encoder.npy')
4.    return label_encoder
```

Resuable function to create the confusion matrix.

```
1. def getClassificationReport(test_labels, prediction):
2.
3.    def plot_confusion_matrix(cm, classes,
4.                              normalize=False,
5.                              title='Confusion matrix',
6.                              cmap=plt.cm.Blues):
7.    """
8.    This function prints and plots the confusion
      matrix.
9.    Normalization can be applied by setting
      `normalize=True`.
10.   """
11.   import itertools
12.   if normalize:
13.       cm = cm.astype('float') / cm.sum(axis=1)[:,
          np.newaxis]
14.       print("Normalized confusion matrix")
15.   else:
16.       print('Confusion matrix, without normalization')
17.
18.   #print(cm)
19.
20.   plt.imshow(cm, interpolation='nearest', cmap=cmap)
21.   plt.title(title)
22.   #plt.colorbar()
23.   tick_marks = np.arange(len(classes))
```

```
24.      plt.xticks(tick_marks, classes, rotation=45)
25.      plt.yticks(tick_marks, classes)
26.
27.      fmt = '.2f' if normalize else 'd'
28.      thresh = cm.max() / 2.
29.      for i, j in itertools.product(range(cm.
         shape[0]), range(cm.shape[1])):
30.          plt.text(j, i, format(cm[i, j], fmt),
31.          horizontalalignment="center",
32.          color="white" if cm[i, j] > thresh else "black")
33.
34.      plt.ylabel('True label')
35.      plt.xlabel('Predicted label')
36.      plt.tight_layout()
37.      plt.show()
38.
39.      from sklearn.metrics import confusion_matrix
40.      test_label_list=list(np.unique(test_labels))
41.      cnf_matrix = confusion_matrix(test_labels,
         prediction,labels=test_label_list)
42.      np.set_printoptions(precision=2)
43.
44.      # Plot non-normalized confusion matrix
45.      plt.figure(figsize=(8,8))
46.      plot_confusion_matrix(cnf_matrix,
         classes=test_label_list,
47.      title='Confusion matrix, without normalization')
48.
49.
50.      from sklearn import metrics
51.
52.      accuracy = round(metrics.accuracy_score(test_
         labels, prediction),3)
53.      precision = round(metrics.precision_score(test_
         labels, prediction, average='weighted'),3)
54.      recall = round(metrics.recall_score(test_labels,
         prediction, average='weighted'),3)
55.      f1_score = round(metrics.f1_score(test_labels,
         prediction, average='weighted'),3)
56.
57.      # Balanced
58.      balanced_accuracy = round(metrics.balanced_
         accuracy_score(test_labels, prediction),3)
59.
60.      FP = cnf_matrix.sum(axis=0) - np.diag(cnf_matrix)
61.      FN = cnf_matrix.sum(axis=1) - np.diag(cnf_matrix)
```

```
62.    TP = np.diag(cnf_matrix)
63.    TN = cnf_matrix.sum() - (FP + FN + TP)
64.
65.    # Sensitivity, hit rate, recall, or true
       positive rate
66.    TPR = round((TP/(TP+FN)).mean(),3)
67.    # Specificity or true negative rate
68.    TNR = round((TN/(TN+FP) ).mean(),3)
69.    # Precision or positive predictive value
70.    PPV = round((TP/(TP+FP)).mean(),3)
71.    # Negative predictive value
72.    NPV = round((TN/(TN+FN)).mean(),3)
73.    # Fall out or false positive rate
74.    FPR = round((FP/(FP+TN)).mean(),3)
75.    # False negative rate
76.    FNR = round((FN/(TP+FN)).mean(),3)
77.    # False discovery rate
78.    FDR = round((FP/(TP+FP)).mean(),3)
79.
80.    # Overall accuracy
81.    Overall_Acc = round((((TP+TN)/(TP+FP+FN+TN)).
       mean(),3)
82.    Bal_F1 = round((2*(PPV*TPR)/(PPV+TPR)),3)
83.
84.
85.    print("Acc= ", accuracy)
86.    print("Pre= ", precision)
87.    print("Rec= ", recall)
88.    print("F1= ", f1_score)
89.    print("")
90.
91.    print("Bal_Acc = ", balanced_accuracy)
92.    print("Bal_Pre = ", PPV)
93.    print("Bal_Rec = ", TPR)
94.    print("Bal_F1= ", Bal_F1)
95.    print("")
96.
97.    from sklearn.metrics import classification_
       report, confusion_matrix
98.    print(classification_report(test_labels,
       prediction))
99.
100.   return accuracy, precision, recall, f1_score,
       balanced_accuracy, PPV, TPR, Bal_F1, TNR, NPV,
       FPR, FNR, FDR, Overall_Acc
101.
```

Reusable function to build the classifier.

```
1.  def classify(model_name, classifier, image_size,
    n_component):
2.    X_train, y_train, X_test, y_test = getData(model_
    name, image_size, n_component)
3.
4.    if classifier == "RF":
5.      from sklearn.ensemble import
    RandomForestClassifier
6.    model = RandomForestClassifier(n_estimators =
    100, random_state = 42)
7.    elif classifier == "SVM":
8.      from sklearn.svm import SVC
9.      model = SVC(kernel='linear', degree=3, C=1,
    decision_function_shape='ovo')
10.
11.   # Train the model on training data
12.   model.fit(X_train, y_train) #For sklearn no one
    hot encoding
13.
14.   #Now predict using the trained RF model.
15.   prediction = model.predict(X_test)
16.
17.   #get the encoder from the pickle file
18.   from sklearn import preprocessing
19.   le = preprocessing.LabelEncoder()
20.   le.classes_ = getLabelEncoder(layer, image_size)
21.
22.   import pickle
23.   model_loc = "models"
24.   filename = model_loc + "/" + layer + "_" +
    preprocessing_technique + "_" + str(n_component)
    + "_" + 'classifier'+ "_" + model_name + "_" +
    classifier + "_" + str(image_size) + ".sav "
25.   pickle.dump(model, open(filename, 'wb'))
26.
27.   #Inverse le transform to get original label back.
28.   prediction = le.inverse_transform(prediction)
29.   y_test = le.inverse_transform(y_test)
30.
31.   accuracy, precision, recall, f1_score, balanced_
    accuracy, PPV, TPR, Bal_F1, TNR, NPV, FPR, FNR,
    FDR, Overall_Acc = getClassificationReport(y_
    test, prediction)
32.   return accuracy, precision, recall, f1_score,
    balanced_accuracy, PPV, TPR, Bal_F1, TNR, NPV,
    FPR, FNR, FDR, Overall_Acc
```

Finally, run the loop.

```
1.  list_of_analysis=[]
2.  for image_size in list_of_size:
3.    for classifier in list_of_classifiers:
4.      for model in list_of_architectures:
5.        for n_component in n_components:
6.          print("---------------------------------
            --------------------------------------------")
7.          print(classifier + " - " + model + " - " +
            str(image_size) + "-" + str(n_component))
8.          print("")
9.          accuracy, precision, recall, f1_score,
            balanced_accuracy, PPV, TPR, Bal_F1, TNR,
            NPV, FPR, FNR, FDR, Overall_Acc =
            classify(model, classifier, image_size,
            n_component)
10.         list_of_analysis.append(
11. [
12.         classifier, model, image_size, n_component,
            accuracy, precision, recall, f1_score,
            balanced_accuracy, PPV, TPR, Bal_F1, TNR,
            NPV, FPR, FNR, FDR, Overall_Acc
13. ]
14. )
15.         list_of_analysis
```

Performance Assessment of Various Experimentations

The reduced dimensional data are further used to build the machine learning classification model using the Random Forest and SVM algorithms (Table 6.2).

Image size – (128, 128, 3), (256, 256, 3)
Classifier – Random Forest, Support Vector Machine
PCA n_components – [50, 100, 500, 1000, 1500]

Summary

In this chapter, we have observed how the same data points represented in higher-dimensional space are represented using lower dimensional planes of 50, 100 and 500 dimensions. Further, the new data points with lower dimensions will be fed into the classification model for performing the image classification task.

TABLE 6.2   Performance Metrics for Classification of PCA'd Data

MODEL	A	ACCURACY	PRECISION	RECALL	F1_SCORE	FPR	IMAGE SIZE	CLASSIFIER
MobileNet	**100**	**0.877**	**0.879**	**0.877**	**0.874**	**0.015**	(128, 128, 3)	RF
VGG19	100	0.865	0.869	0.865	0.863	0.016	(128, 128, 3)	RF
MobileNet	500	0.865	0.866	0.865	0.861	0.016	(128, 128, 3)	RF
MobileNet	**500**	**0.884**	**0.884**	**0.884**	**0.88**	**0.014**	(128, 128, 3)	SVM
MobileNetV2	500	0.859	0.866	0.859	0.858	0.016	(128, 128, 3)	SVM
DenseNet201	500	0.837	0.843	0.837	0.837	0.018	(128, 128, 3)	SVM
DenseNet169	**100**	**0.883**	**0.883**	**0.883**	**0.88**	**0.015**	(256, 256, 3)	RF
VGG16	100	0.88	0.884	0.88	0.877	0.015	(256, 256, 3)	RF
MobileNet	500	0.878	0.877	0.878	0.871	0.017	(256, 256, 3)	RF
DenseNet201	**500**	**0.897**	**0.899**	**0.897**	**0.896**	**0.013**	(256, 256, 3)	SVM
DenseNet169	500	0.892	0.894	0.892	0.891	0.013	(256, 256, 3)	SVM
VGG16	500	0.888	0.889	0.888	0.886	0.014	(256, 256, 3)	SVM

The bold signifies the best results in various techniques in the table.

Feature Fusion Techniques

7

Features from images can be extracted using handcrafted techniques like HOG (Li et al., 2016), SURF (Bay et al., 2006), SIFT (Wu et al., 2013), DAISY (Tola et al., 2010), and so on. Features can be extracted using SOTA CNN models like Inception (Szegedy et al., 2015), RestNet (He et al., 2016), DenseNet (Huang et al., 2017), and so on. Now, these features are extracted from the same image, just that they are different representations of the same image extracted using different techniques. Every feature representation extracted from an image using various techniques has its own strength. Some representations can perform better than others when it comes to classifying images. In this chapter, we will see how we can fuse different image representations, to generate even more robust representations of an image.

STRUCTURE

In this chapter, we will cover the following topics:

- Basics of feature fusion technique
- Different combinations of image representations
- Different feature fusion approaches
- Classification model using fused features

DOI: 10.1201/9781003217381-7

OBJECTIVE

After studying this chapter, you should be able to fuse features generated using different image representation techniques. You will be aware of how features can be fused in a combination of two and three different representations. Additionally, you will learn how to fuse features both horizontally and vertically. Finally, classification models will be created for all different fused features.

BASICS OF FEATURE FUSION TECHNIQUE

Feature fusion (Gao & Chen, 2017) is a technique to concatenate the features extracted from the same image, but using different algorithms. In our study, since we will extract features from the same set of images using different CNN applications, we will experiment with fusing the features extracted from CNN applications, and evaluate if fusing the features extracted from different algorithms results in better performance as compared to results obtained from the individual CNN application features.

In previous chapters, we extracted features from the CNN applications and used those features to build a classifier; hence we will experiment with fusion of these features. Features extracted from an image are basically a representation of the image. Using various techniques to extract features from the same image is basically different feature representations of the same image.

Feature fusion is the technique to merge, either horizontally or vertically, the various representations of the image to form a different feature representation of the same image.

We experimented with fusing features extracted using various CNN applications like VGGNet, ResNet, DenseNet, and so on. We fused the features formed after treating class imbalance using SMOTE (Chawla et al., 2002). Additionally, we also experimented with fusing features after dimensionality reduction using PCA.

Since features extracted from different CNN models are of different dimensions, vertical fusion of those features cannot be performed. Hence, vertical fusion was performed only for PCA'd data, as we convert the features to the same dimensions while performing PCA. In our experiment, we reduced the dimensions of all the extracted features to 50, 100, 500 dimensions.

Different Combinations of Image Representations

Python code for generating combinations of two architectures.

```
1. from itertools import combinations
2. list_of_combinations=[",".join(map(str, comb)) for
   comb in combinations(list_of_architectures, 2)]
3. print(list_of_combinations)
```

This will generate all the combinations displayed below.

```
['Xception,VGG16',
 'Xception,VGG19',
 'Xception,ResNet50',
 'Xception,ResNet101',
 'Xception,ResNet152',
 'Xception,ResNet50V2',
 'Xception,ResNet101V2',
 'Xception,ResNet152V2',
 'Xception,InceptionV3',
 'Xception,InceptionResNetV2',
 'Xception,MobileNet',
 'Xception,MobileNetV2',
 'Xception,DenseNet121',
 'Xception,DenseNet169',
 'Xception,DenseNet201',
 'VGG16,VGG19',
 'VGG16,ResNet50',
 'VGG16,ResNet101',
 'VGG16,ResNet152',
 'VGG16,ResNet50V2',
 'VGG16,ResNet101V2',
 'VGG16,ResNet152V2',
 'VGG16,InceptionV3',
 'VGG16,InceptionResNetV2',
 'VGG16,MobileNet',
```

Python code for generating combinations of three architectures.

```
1. from itertools import combinations
2. list_of_combinations=[",".join(map(str, comb)) for
   comb in combinations(list_of_architectures, 3)]
3. print(list_of_combinations)
```

This will generate all the combinations displayed below.

```
['Xception,VGG16,VGG19',
 'Xception,VGG16,ResNet50',
 'Xception,VGG16,ResNet101',
 'Xception,VGG16,ResNet152',
 'Xception,VGG16,ResNet50V2',
 'Xception,VGG16,ResNet101V2',
 'Xception,VGG16,ResNet152V2',
 'Xception,VGG16,InceptionV3',
 'Xception,VGG16,InceptionResNetV2',
 'Xception,VGG16,MobileNet',
 'Xception,VGG16,MobileNetV2',
 'Xception,VGG16,DenseNet121',
 'Xception,VGG16,DenseNet169',
 'Xception,VGG16,DenseNet201',
 'Xception,VGG19,ResNet50',
 'Xception,VGG19,ResNet101',
 'Xception,VGG19,ResNet152',
 'Xception,VGG19,ResNet50V2',
 'Xception,VGG19,ResNet101V2',
 'Xception,VGG19,ResNet152V2',
 'Xception,VGG19,InceptionV3',
 'Xception,VGG19,InceptionResNetV2',
 'Xception,VGG19,MobileNet',
 'Xception,VGG19,MobileNetV2',
 'Xception,VGG19,DenseNet121',
 'Xception,VGG19,DenseNet169',
 'Xception,VGG19,DenseNet201',
 'Xception,ResNet50,ResNet101',
 'Xception,ResNet50,ResNet152',
 'Xception,ResNet50,ResNet50V2',
 'Xception,ResNet50,ResNet101V2',
 'Xception,ResNet50,ResNet152V2',
 'Xception,ResNet50,InceptionV3',
 'Xception,ResNet50,InceptionResNetV2',
 'Xception,ResNet50,MobileNet',
 'Xception,ResNet50,MobileNetV2',
 'Xception,ResNet50,DenseNet121',
 'Xception,ResNet50,DenseNet169',
 'Xception,ResNet50,DenseNet201',
```

DIFFERENT FEATURE FUSION APPROACHES

Fusing Features Horizontally Extracted from the Last Convolution Layer and after Treating Class Imbalance in a Combination of Two CNN Models

In this approach, once the features are extracted from the CNN applications, features are fused in a combination of two CNN applications. Since the dimensions of the features extracted from different CNN applications are different, vertical fusion of these features cannot be conducted (Figure 7.1).

Python implementation of the technique.

```
1. import tensorflow as tf
2. def getData(model1, model2, image_size):
3.     train_data_dir="../class_imabalance/" + layer +
       "/" + str(image_size)+"/"
4.     test_data_dir="../feature_extractor/" + layer +
       "/" + str(image_size)+"/"
5.     X_train1=np.load(train_data_dir+model1+"_X_
       train_SMOTE.npy")
6.     X_train2=np.load(train_data_dir+model2+"_X_
       train_SMOTE.npy")
7.     X_train = tf.keras.layers.concatenate([X_train1,
       X_train2],
8.     axis=1)
9.     y_train=np.load(train_data_dir+model1+"_y_train_
       SMOTE.npy")
10.    X_test1=np.load(test_data_dir+model1+"_test_
       images.npy")
11.    X_test2=np.load(test_data_dir+model2+"_test_
       images.npy")
12.    X_test = tf.keras.layers.concatenate([X_test1,
       X_test2],
13.    axis=1)
14.    y_test=np.load(test_data_dir+"test_labels.npy")
15.    return X_train, y_train, X_test, y_test
```

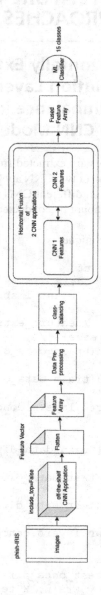

FIGURE 7.1 Horizonal feature fusion of SMOTE-treated data for two CNN applications.

Fusing Features Horizontally Extracted from the Last Convolution Layer and after Treating Class Imbalance in a Combination of Three CNN Models

In this approach, once the features are extracted from the CNN applications, they are fused horizontally in a combination of three CNN applications (Figure 7.2).

Python implementation of the technique.

```
1. import tensorflow as tf
2. def getData(model1, model2, model3, image_size):
3.     train_data_dir="../class_imabalance/" + layer +
       "/" + str(image_size)+"/"
4.     test_data_dir="../feature_extractor/" + layer +
       "/" + str(image_size)+"/"
5.     X_train1=np.load(train_data_dir+model1+"_X_
       train_SMOTE.npy")
6.     X_train2=np.load(train_data_dir+model2+"_X_
       train_SMOTE.npy")
7.     X_train3=np.load(train_data_dir+model3+"_X_
       train_SMOTE.npy")
8.     X_train = tf.keras.layers.concatenate([X_train1,
       X_train2, X_train3],
9.     axis=1)
10.    y_train=np.load(train_data_dir+model1+"_y_train_
       SMOTE.npy")
11.    X_test1=np.load(test_data_dir+model1+"_test_
       images.npy")
12.    X_test2=np.load(test_data_dir+model2+"_test_
       images.npy")
13.    X_test3=np.load(test_data_dir+model3+"_test_
       images.npy")
14.    X_test = tf.keras.layers.concatenate([X_test1,
       X_test2, X_test3],
15.    axis=1)
16.    y_test=np.load(test_data_dir+"test_labels.npy")
17.    return X_train, y_train, X_test, y_test
```

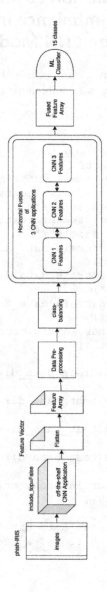

FIGURE 7.2   Horizonal feature fusion of SMOTE-treated data for three CNN applications.

Fusing PCA'd Features Horizontally Extracted from the Last Convolution Layer and Class Imbalance Treatment in a Combination of Two CNN Models

Fusing PCA'd data will result in the same dimensional data for all the applications, since after PCA treatment of the data, all the feature arrays from different applications are now of the same dimension (Figure 7.3).

For example, features are extracted from the Xception or VGG16 applications; after PCA the dimensions of the data are the same for both of them. In the case of reducing the dimensions to 50, both the arrays have 50 columns now.

Hence, fusing them with each other will result in the same dimensional data for all applications. Additionally, since they are horizontally fused, the number of records will remain the same, in this case 6000, but the number of columns will be added based on the number of applications fused, which is 2 in this case.

Python implementation of the technique.

```
1. import tensorflow as tf
2. def getData(model1, model2, image_size, n_component):
3.     X_data_dir="../pca/" + layer + "/" +
       str(image_size)+"/"
4.     y_train_data_dir="../class_imabalance/" + layer +
       "/" + str(image_size)+"/"
5.     y_test_data_dir="../feature_extractor/" + layer +
       "/" + str(image_size)+"/"
6.     X_train1=np.load(X_data_dir+model1+"_train_" +
       str(n_component) + ".npy")
7.     X_train2=np.load(X_data_dir+model2+"_train_" +
       str(n_component) + ".npy")
8.     X_train = tf.keras.layers.concatenate([X_train1,
       X_train2],
9.     axis=1)
10.    y_train=np.load(y_train_data_dir+model1+"_y_
       train_SMOTE.npy")
11.    X_test1=np.load(X_data_dir+model1+"_test_" +
       str(n_component) + ".npy")
12.    X_test2=np.load(X_data_dir+model2+"_test_" +
       str(n_component) + ".npy")
13.    X_test = tf.keras.layers.concatenate([X_test1,
       X_test2],
14.    axis=1)
15.    y_test=np.load(y_test_data_dir+"test_labels.npy")
16.    return X_train, y_train, X_test, y_test
```

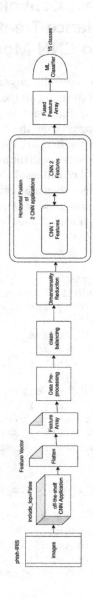

FIGURE 7.3   Horizonal feature fusion of PCA treated data for two CNN applications.

Fusing PCA'd Features Horizontally Extracted from the Last Convolution Layer and Class Imbalance Treatment in a Combination of Three CNN Models

Python implementation of the technique (Figure 7.4).

```
1. import tensorflow as tf
2. def getData(model1, model2, model3, image_size,
   n_component):
3.     X_data_dir="../pca/" + layer + "/" +
       str(image_size)+"/"
4.     y_train_data_dir="../class_imabalance/" + layer +
       "/" + str(image_size)+"/"
5.     y_test_data_dir="../feature_extractor/" + layer +
       "/" + str(image_size)+"/"
6.     X_train1=np.load(X_data_dir+model1+"_train_" +
       str(n_component) + ".npy")
7.     X_train2=np.load(X_data_dir+model2+"_train_" +
       str(n_component) + ".npy")
8.     X_train3=np.load(X_data_dir+model3+"_train_" +
       str(n_component) + ".npy")
9.     X_train = tf.keras.layers.concatenate([X_train1,
       X_train2, X_train3],
10.    axis=1)
11.    y_train=np.load(y_train_data_dir+model1+"_y_
       train_SMOTE.npy")
12.    X_test1=np.load(X_data_dir+model1+"_test_" +
       str(n_component) + ".npy")
13.    X_test2=np.load(X_data_dir+model2+"_test_" +
       str(n_component) + ".npy")
14.    X_test3=np.load(X_data_dir+model3+"_test_" +
       str(n_component) + ".npy")
15.    X_test = tf.keras.layers.concatenate([X_test1,
       X_test2, X_test3],
16.    axis=1)
17.    y_test=np.load(y_test_data_dir+"test_labels.npy")
18.    return X_train, y_train, X_test, y_test
```

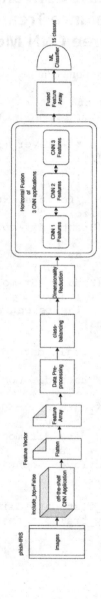

FIGURE 7.4 Horizonal feature fusion of PCA treated data for three CNN applications.

Fusing PCA'd Features Vertically Extracted from the Last Convolution Layer and Class Imbalance Treatment in a Combination of Two CNN Models

In this section, we will discuss the vertical fusion of the PCA'd data for all the applications in a combination of two CNN applications. With the same argument as explained in the section where fusion of PCA'd data is performed, fusing them among each other will result in the same dimensional data for all the applications (Figure 7.5).

Additionally, since they are vertically fused, the number of columns will remain the same, in this case 50, 100 or 500 based on the PCA'd data used for the fusion, but the number of records will be added based on the number of application data fused, which is two in this case.

Python implementation of the technique.

```
1. import tensorflow as tf
2. def getData(model1, model2, image_size,
   n_component):
3.    X_data_dir=".../pca/" + layer + "/" +
      str(image_size)+"/"
4.    y_train_data_dir=".../class_imabalance/" + layer +
      "/" + str(image_size)+"/"
5.    y_test_data_dir=".../feature_extractor/" + layer +
      "/" + str(image_size)+"/"
6.    X_train1=np.load(X_data_dir+model1+"_train_" +
      str(n_component) + ".npy")
7.    X_train2=np.load(X_data_dir+model2+"_train_" +
      str(n_component) + ".npy")
8.    X_train = tf.keras.layers.concatenate([X_train1,
      X_train2],
9.    axis=0)
10.   y_train1=np.load(y_train_data_dir+model1+"_y_
      train_SMOTE.npy")
11.   y_train2=np.load(y_train_data_dir+model2+"_y_
      train_SMOTE.npy")
12.   y_train = tf.keras.layers.concatenate([y_train1,
      y_train2],
13.   axis=0)
14.   X_test1=np.load(X_data_dir+model1+"_test_" +
      str(n_component) + ".npy")
```

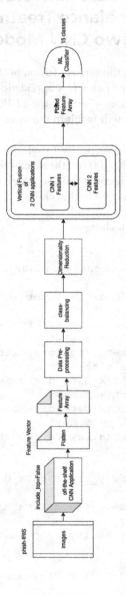

FIGURE 7.5   Vertical feature fusion of PCA treated data for two CNN applications.

```
15.    X_test2=np.load(X_data_dir+model2+"_test_" +
       str(n_component) + ".npy")
16.    X_test = tf.keras.layers.concatenate([X_test1,
       X_test2],
17.    axis=0)
18.    y_test1=np.load(y_test_data_dir+"test_labels.npy")
19.    y_test2=np.load(y_test_data_dir+"test_labels.npy")
20.    y_test = tf.keras.layers.concatenate([y_test1,
       y_test2],
21.    axis=0)
22.    return X_train, y_train, X_test, y_test
```

Fusing PCA'd Features Vertically Extracted from the Last Convolution Layer and Class Imbalance Treatment in a Combination of Three CNN Models

Python implementation of the technique (Figure 7.6).

```
1.  import tensorflow as tf
2.  def getData(model1, model2, model3, image_size,
    n_component):
3.      X_data_dir="../pca/" + layer + "/" +
        str(image_size)+"/"
4.      y_train_data_dir="../class_imabalance/" + layer +
        "/" + str(image_size)+"/"
5.      y_test_data_dir="../feature_extractor/" + layer +
        "/" + str(image_size)+"/"
6.      X_train1=np.load(X_data_dir+model1+"_train_" +
        str(n_component) + ".npy")
7.      X_train2=np.load(X_data_dir+model2+"_train_" +
        str(n_component) + ".npy")
8.      X_train3=np.load(X_data_dir+model3+"_train_" +
        str(n_component) + ".npy")
9.      X_train = tf.keras.layers.concatenate([X_train1,
        X_train2, X_train3],
10.     axis=0)
11.     y_train1=np.load(y_train_data_dir+model1+"_y_
        train_SMOTE.npy")
12.     y_train = tf.keras.layers.concatenate([y_train1,
        y_train1, y_train1],
```

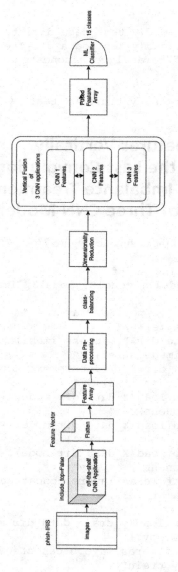

FIGURE 7.6 Vertical feature fusion of PCA treated data for three CNN applications.

```
13.   axis=0)
14.   X_test1=np.load(X_data_dir+model1+"_test_" +
      str(n_component) + ".npy")
15.   X_test2=np.load(X_data_dir+model2+"_test_" +
      str(n_component) + ".npy")
16.   X_test3=np.load(X_data_dir+model3+"_test_" +
      str(n_component) + ".npy")
17.   X_test = tf.keras.layers.concatenate([X_test1,
      X_test2, X_test3],
18.   axis=0)
19.   y_test1=np.load(y_test_data_dir+"test_labels.
      npy")
20.   y_test = tf.keras.layers.concatenate([y_test1,
      y_test1, y_test1],
21.   axis=0)
22.   return X_train, y_train, X_test, y_test
```

Performance Assessment of Various Experimentations

We performed various experimentations using various different feature fusion techniques. The table below demonstrates the comparison of all the tried approaches to provide a holistic view of the results achieved.
See Table 7.1.

Summary

In this chapter, we experimented with fused features generated by combining image representations in a combination of two and three CNN architectures. Additionally, features were fused both horizontally and vertically before feeding them into different classification models.

TABLE 7.1   Performance Assessment of Models Built Using Feature Fusion Techniques

MODEL 1	MODEL 2	MODEL 3	N	ACCURACY	PRECISION	RECALL	F1_SCORE	FPR	IMAGE SIZE	FUSION TYPE
VGG19	**DenseNet169**			**0.884**	**0.888**	**0.884**	**0.883**	**0.014**	128	Vertical
VGG16	MobileNet			0.882	0.885	0.882	0.879	0.014	128	Vertical
Xception	**DenseNet201**			**0.895**	**0.894**	**0.895**	**0.891**	**0.015**	256	Vertical
ResNet50V2	DenseNet201			0.895	0.894	0.895	0.889	0.015	256	Vertical
ResNet101V2	**MobileNetV2**	**DenseNet201**		**0.89**	**0.891**	**0.89**	**0.888**	**0.013**	128	Vertical
MobileNet	MobileNetV2	DenseNet201		0.887	0.889	0.887	0.885	0.013	128	Vertical
VGG19	**ResNet152V2**	**DenseNet201**		**0.897**	**0.895**	**0.897**	**0.893**	**0.014**	256	Vertical
VGG16	ResNet152V2	DenseNet201		0.893	0.895	0.893	0.89	0.014	256	Vertical
VGG16	**MobileNetV2**		**100**	**0.855**	**0.861**	**0.855**	**0.853**	**0.017**	128	Horizontal
VGG16	DenseNet201		100	0.855	0.856	0.855	0.853	0.017	128	Horizontal
VGG19	DenseNet169		100	0.854	0.856	0.854	0.852	0.017	128	Horizontal
VGG16	**DenseNet169**	**DenseNet201**	**100**	**0.875**	**0.877**	**0.875**	**0.871**	**0.015**	256	Horizontal
VGG16	MobileNet		100	0.87	0.874	0.87	0.867	0.016	256	Horizontal
VGG16	DenseNet121		100	0.87	0.871	0.87	0.866	0.016	256	Horizontal
MobileNet	**MobileNetV2**	**DenseNet201**	**100**	**0.873**	**0.88**	**0.873**	**0.873**	**0.013**	128	Horizontal
VGG16	MobileNet	DenseNet201	100	0.868	0.879	0.868	0.869	0.013	128	Horizontal
VGG16	MobileNet	DenseNet121	100	0.867	0.878	0.867	0.869	0.013	128	Horizontal
MobileNetV2	**DenseNet169**	**DenseNet201**	**100**	**0.88**	**0.887**	**0.88**	**0.881**	**0.012**	256	Horizontal
VGG16	ResNet152V2	DenseNet169	100	0.878	0.883	0.878	0.877	0.012	256	Horizontal
VGG16	InceptionV3	DenseNet169	100	0.877	0.886	0.877	0.877	0.013	256	Horizontal
VGG16	**MobileNetV2**		**100**	**0.855**	**0.861**	**0.855**	**0.853**	**0.017**	128	Vertical

(Continued)

TABLE 7.1 (CONTINUED)   Performance Assessment of Models Built Using Feature Fusion Techniques

MODEL 1	MODEL 2	MODEL 3	N	ACCURACY	PRECISION	RECALL	F1_SCORE	FPR	IMAGE SIZE	FUSION TYPE
VGG16	DenseNet201		100	0.855	0.856	0.855	0.853	0.017	128	Vertical
VGG19	DenseNet169		100	0.854	0.856	0.854	0.852	0.017	128	Vertical
VGG16	**DenseNet169**		**100**	**0.875**	**0.877**	**0.875**	**0.871**	**0.015**	256	Vertical
VGG16	MobileNet		100	0.87	0.874	0.87	0.867	0.016	256	Vertical
VGG16	DenseNet121		100	0.87	0.871	0.87	0.866	0.016	256	Vertical
VGG16	**MobileNetV2**	**DenseNet169**	**100**	**0.85**	**0.855**	**0.85**	**0.847**	**0.019**	128	Vertical
VGG19	MobileNet	MobileNetV2	100	0.848	0.852	0.848	0.846	0.017	128	Vertical
VGG16	MobileNetV2	DenseNet201	100	0.847	0.849	0.847	0.844	0.018	128	Vertical
VGG16	**MobileNetV2**	**DenseNet169**	**100**	**0.869**	**0.869**	**0.869**	**0.864**	**0.018**	256	Vertical
VGG19	MobileNet	DenseNet121	100	0.867	0.869	0.867	0.862	0.017	256	Vertical
VGG16	MobileNet	DenseNet121	100	0.866	0.866	0.866	0.862	0.017	256	Vertical

The bold signifies the best results in the table.

Comparison of Phishing Detection Approaches

8

This chapter looks into the implementation outcomes of the various approaches and techniques used for building and evaluating the phish-IRIS dataset-based classification model. Numerous classification models within each suggested approach are built and experimented with various combinations with data dimensions and fusions. In this chapter, a comparison of how each approach has performed and how they perform against state-of-the-art performance with this dataset is conducted.

CLASSIFICATION APPROACHES

Table 8.1 lists all the different approaches suggested in this book.

EVALUATION OF CLASSIFICATION EXPERIMENTS

Images in the phish-IRIS dataset are resized into three different dimensions: (128, 128, 3), (256, 256, 3) and (512, 512, 3). Features are extracted utilizing CNN applications like VGGNet, DenseNet, and so on, for all the image sizes. Additionally, dimensionality reduction and feature fusion of the extracted

DOI: 10.1201/9781003217381-8

TABLE 8.1   Description of All the Classification Approaches Proposed in
This Book

APPROACHES	DESCRIPTION
Approach 1	Traditional CNN with image size of (128, 128, 3) and (256, 256, 3)
Approach 2	Transfer the learning till last fully connected layer
Approach 3	Transfer the learning till last convolution layer, extract features and SMOTE, and implement a machine learning classifier
Approach 4	Horizontal fusion of the features extracted in Approach 3 in a combination of two and three CNN applications
Approach 5	PCA of the features extracted in Approach 3 and implement a machine learning classifier
Approach 6	Horizontal fusion of the features extracted in Approach 5 in a combination of two and three CNN applications
Approach 7	Vertical fusion of the features extracted in Approach 5 in a combination of two and three CNN applications
Approach 8	Apply RF and SVM on the best performing model from all the above approaches for an image size of (512, 512, 3)

features are done to build numerous classification models. Table 8.2 lists all the best performing models within each approach experimented in this book. The table is sorted by recall (TPR) value against each experiment.

As can be seen in Table 8.2, the classifier built from features extracted using DenseNet201 for the image size of (512, 512, 3) performed exceptionally well when trained using the SVM classification algorithm.

For a multi-class classification model, the performance of the DenseNet201-based model against each class is shown in Figure 5.1, and the confusion matrix is shown in Figure 5.2 (Figures 8.1 and 8.2).

Comparison of the Best Performing Model with the State-of-the-Art Technique

State-of-the-art performance of a machine learning-based classifier for the phish-IRIS dataset provided in their official site (*Phish-IRIS Dataset – A Small Scale Multi-Class Phishing Web Page Screenshots Archive*, n.d.) is explored to compare the best performing model implemented in this chapter, as shown in Table 8.3.

Performance metrics of all the approaches conducted in this study as per Table 8.2, along with the state-of-the-art results against True Positive Rate (Recall) values, are shown in Figure 8.3.

TABLE 8.2 Comparison of the Best Performing Models within Different Approaches

APPROACH	MODEL	RECALL	F1	IMAGE SIZE	CLASSIFIER
8	**DenseNet201**	**0.908**	**0.909**	**512**	**SVM**
3	DenseNet201	0.903	0.903	256	SVM
3	DenseNet201	0.897	0.89	256	RF
4	VGG19_ResNet152V2_DenseNet201	0.897	0.893	256	RF
5	DenseNet201_500	0.897	0.896	256	SVM
4	Xception_DenseNet201	0.895	0.891	256	RF
3	MobileNet	0.891	0.89	128	SVM
4	ResNet101V2_MobileNetV2_DenseNet201	0.89	0.888	128	RF
3	VGG16	0.885	0.88	128	RF
5	MobileNet_500	0.884	0.88	128	SVM
4	VGG19_DenseNet169	0.884	0.883	128	RF
5	DenseNet169_100	0.883	0.88	256	RF
6	MobileNetV2_DenseNet169_DenseNet201_100	0.88	0.881	256	RF
5	MobileNet_100	0.877	0.874	128	RF
7	VGG16_DenseNet169_100	0.875	0.871	256	RF
6	VGG16_DenseNet169_100	0.875	0.871	256	RF
6	MobileNet_MobileNetV2_DenseNet201_100	0.873	0.873	128	RF
7	VGG16_MobileNetV2_DenseNet169_100	0.869	0.864	256	RF
2	DenseNet169	0.869	0.884	256	NN
6	VGG16_MobileNetV2_100	0.855	0.853	128	RF
7	VGG16_MobileNetV2_100	0.855	0.853	128	RF
7	VGG16_MobileNetV2_DenseNet169_100	0.85	0.847	128	RF
2	DenseNet169	0.791	0.825	128	NN

	precision	recall	f1-score	support
adobe	0.77	0.89	0.83	27
alibaba	1.00	0.85	0.92	26
amazon	0.67	0.36	0.47	11
apple	1.00	0.87	0.93	15
boa	0.83	0.97	0.89	35
chase	0.86	0.86	0.86	37
dhl	1.00	0.90	0.95	42
dropbox	0.89	0.85	0.87	40
facebook	0.86	0.75	0.80	57
linkedin	1.00	0.64	0.78	14
microsoft	0.92	0.68	0.78	53
other	0.94	0.96	0.95	1000
paypal	0.78	0.73	0.76	93
wellsfargo	0.65	0.82	0.73	45
yahoo	0.95	0.89	0.92	44
accuracy			0.91	1539
macro avg	0.88	0.80	0.83	1539
weighted avg	0.91	0.91	0.91	1539

FIGURE 8.1   Performance metrics for DenseNet201 against each class.

Performance metrics of all the approaches conducted in this study as per Table 8.2, along with the state-of-the-art results against F1 score values, are shown in Figure 8.4.

As can be seen from Figures 5.4 and 5.5, the results yielded by SVM over features extracted via the DenseNet201 CNN model for the image size of (512, 512, 3) exceed the state-of-the-art performance for this dataset.

Summary

The evaluation of a classification model requires an understanding of the problem statement so that relevant performance metrics can be chosen. In the case of phishing detection, True Positive Rate is a better evaluation metric, which means that it is more important for the classification model to predict all of the phishing websites as "phishing", even if that results in classifying few legitimate websites as "phishing". At the same time, it is also important for a classification model to limit the number of legitimate websites as "phishing"; hence False Positive Rate is another important metric for evaluation. Based on the relevant performance metrics, the results of the various

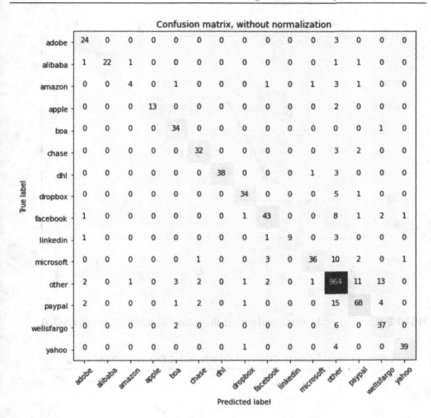

FIGURE 8.2 Confusion matrix for DenseNet201.

TABLE 8.3 Comparison of Best Models with SOTA

METRICS	PHISH-IRIS SOTA	DENSENET201-SVM-512
True positive rate	90.60%	90.80%
False positive rate	8.50%	1.20%
F1 – measure	90.50%	90.60%

approaches implemented in this book are analyzed. It has been observed that the DenseNet201 model, when trained on an image size of (512, 512, 3) using SVM, produces the best results. Additionally, the best performing model is compared against the state-of-the-art performance of the dataset used in this study.

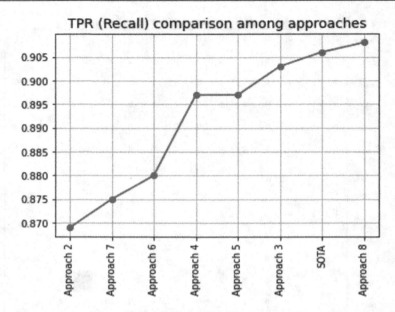

FIGURE 8.3   Comparison based on recall among all approaches and SOTA.

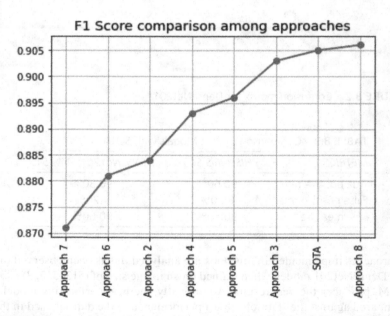

FIGURE 8.4   Comparison based on F1 score among all approaches and SOTA.

Basics of Digital Image Processing 9

Vision is the most important capability that helps us navigate the physical world. We all know that when light falls on an object and gets reflected, the reflection is picked up by the eye, and the information about the object is passed to the brain, the biological neural network, which finally deciphers the object in view. This helps us differentiate between various objects, such as a car and a motorcycle. It helps us to drive the car on a busy road.

Computer vision also follows a similar mechanism as biological vision. With the advancement in computer vision technology, computers can now view the physical world as we do, and can solve similar problems as a human does.

As humans, we solve various kinds of problems on a day-to-day basis, without even appreciating the incredible cognitive capability of the human body and the brain. With computer vision technology, we envisage replicating similar capabilities in computers as in humans. In some cases, we replicate the human capabilities, in others we augment the human capabilities and in still others we surpass the human capabilities.

With our vision, we are capable of differentiating between a dog, a cat and a person. With computer vision, and by using artificial neural networks, the computer can be trained to do the same. This comes under the category of computers replicating human capabilities.

However, if computers are enabled to drive a car, such as in the case of self-driving cars, they are able to not only match but also far surpass human capabilities. It is because computers can have a 360-degree view of the road, see blind spots, and so on, which we cannot replicate.

Now, meeting and surpassing human vision capabilities are good, but training the computers to interpret something that human eyes simply cannot, like detecting a phishing website rather than a legitimate one, is better. Human eyes can be deceived by phishing websites since they look absolutely similar to their legitimate counterparts. Hence, humans get easily trapped in phishing attacks, but using computer vision techniques, we can train the computer to extract features from the image of the phishing website, and train a model to differentiate a phishing website from a legitimate one.

DOI: 10.1201/9781003217381-9

STRUCTURE

In this chapter, we will cover the following topics:

- Basics of digital image processing
- Basics of extracting features using OpenCV

OBJECTIVE

After studying this chapter, you should be aware of the basics of digital image processing. You will be familiar with image filtering concepts and how to extract relevant features from images for further processing.

BASICS OF DIGITAL IMAGE PROCESSING

To understand digital image processing, it's imperative to first understand what a digital image is. When an image is captured, certain information about the object in the image is captured by the camera or a similar device that can capture the image. When the image is processed, the information captured is extracted and then processed.

What Is a Digital Image?

A picture element, usually called "pixels", is the smallest element of a digital image. An image is an arrangement of pixels in n dimensions.

There are two color schemes in an image:

1. Grayscale image
2. RGB (color) image

Grayscale images are what we call black and white images. In such images, each pixel has only one layer. And each pixel has a number associated with it. If it's an 8-bit pixel, the number ranges from 0 to 255. And the number represents intensity, for example the greater the number, the more the intensity. Hence, 0 represents black, and 255 represents white. Hence, a grayscale image can be represented by a single matrix.

For an RGB image, each pixel has three layers. One layer for red, one for green and one for blue. All other colors can be created by adding these three colors in different intensities. Hence, every pixel in an image can be represented with three numbers in each layer of RGB. And hence a color image can be represented by three matrices, one for each layer, with different intensities for each color.

Based on this understanding, if a pixel is defined as a tuple of three elements, wherein the first element is the intensity of red in a pixel, the second element is the intensity of green in a pixel and the third element is the intensity of blue in a pixel, then a pixel which is red in color can be defined as (255,0,0), which means that the intensity of red is 255 and the intensities of green and blue are 0. Hence, this pixel is pure red. Similarly, a pure green pixel can be defined as (0,255,0), and a pure blue pixel can be defined as (0,0,255) (Figure 9.1).

Since an image is a collection of pixels, every image can be defined as a matrix of pixel values. To understand this better, look at Figure 9.2.

As you can see, what we see as a whole image, the computer sees as a pixel representation. The number in the pixel representation is the intensity of white in that particular pixel in the image. Since it's a grayscale image, there is just one channel, and hence one number in that pixel position. In the case of a color image, there will be three numbers in each pixel position, representing the intensity of red, blue and green in their respective channels.

Loading and Displaying Images

The first and foremost thing to be done for a computer to process the image is to load the image in the computer memory, which basically means loading the matrix holding the pixel values of the image into the memory.

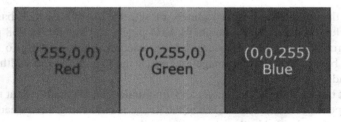

FIGURE 9.1 Pixel layers within digital images.

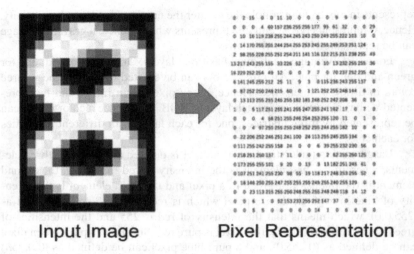

Input Image   **Pixel Representation**

FIGURE 9.2   Pixel representation of a greyscale image.

To do so, let's first import the required libraries.

```
1. from matplotlib import pyplot as plt
2. import cv2
```

Read the image using the imread method in the opencv library.

```
3. image_loc="einstein.png"
4. image = cv2.imread(image_loc)
5. image.shape
```

Note the shape of the image, which is represented as (height, width, channel), which means height at index 0, width at index 1 and channel at index 2.

```
(1034, 968, 3)
```

Hence, the image is read as a matrix of size (1034, 968), which basically means that the image has a height of 1034 pixels and a width of 968 pixels, and there are three such matrices, one for each channel of RGB. To understand it better, let's plot the image and check the height and the width along the x and y axes.

But before we plot the image, let's first understand a small caveat related to the opencv imread module. When the image is read using the imread module, the matrix loaded in the image object is loaded as a numpy array.

This array has 1034 rows, which is the height of the image.

```
1. print(len(image))
```

1034

If we just look at the first row of this matrix, it will contain 968 columns, which is the width of the image.

```
1. print(len(image[0]))
```

968

Hence, an individual pixel will represent three values, one for each RGB channel.

```
1. image[0][0]
```

array([30, 31, 29], dtype=uint8)

However, the opencv library by default reads the image as BGR channel. So, the pixel value represented above basically means that the first pixel of the image has the value of 30 in the blue channel, 31 in the green channel and 29 in the red channel.

Hence, for further processing, there is a need to correct this channel values setting in the numpy array, which holds the image pixel values, which is done using the below code line.

```
1. image = cv2.cvtColor(image, cv2.COLOR_BGR2RGB)
```

Now, if we check the pixel values representation with the array, it will show in the RGB format, which means that the pixel values of each channel remain the same, but they are arranged differently. Earlier it was [B = 30, G = 31, R = 29] and after conversion it became [R = 29, G = 31, B = 30].

```
1. image[0][0]
```

array([29, 31, 30], dtype=uint8)

Let's now plot the image to check the pixel arrangements in the x and y axes (Figure 9.3).

```
2. plt.imshow(image)
3. plt.title("Einstein")
```

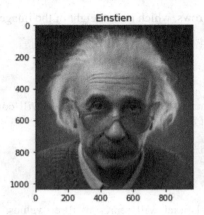

FIGURE 9.3   Pixel representation of a digital image.

```
4. plt.grid(False)
5. plt.show()
```

So, we can see that the image has 1034 pixels vertically along the y axis, which is termed as height, and 968 pixels horizontally along the x axis, which is termed as width, and at every pixel there are three values, one value for the red channel, one value for the green channel and one value for the blue channel.

Hence, the total number of pixel values across the three channels of the image is equal to

$$1034 \times 968 \times 3 = 30,02,736$$

So, what a human eye sees as just an image, a computer sees as 30,02,736 numbers arranged in a defined order.

References

Abdelnabi, Sahar, Krombholz, Katharina, & Fritz, Mario (2020) VisualPhishNet: Zero-day phishing website detection by visual similarity (arxiv.org).

Afroz, S., & Greenstadt, R. (2011). PhishZoo: Detecting Phishing websites by looking at them. *Proceedings – 5th IEEE International Conference on Semantic Computing, ICSC 2011*, 368–375. https://doi.org/10.1109/ICSC.2011.52

Bay, H., Tuytelaars, T., & Gool, L. Van. (2006). LNCS 3951 – SURF: Speeded up robust features. *Computer Vision–ECCV 2006*, 404–417. http://link.springer.com/chapter/10.1007/11744023_32

Bozkir, A. S., & Sezer, E. A. (2016). Use of HOG descriptors in phishing detection. *2016 4th International Symposium on Digital Forensic and Security (ISDFS), 2013*, 148–153. https://doi.org/10.1109/ISDFS.2016.7473534

Bozkır, A. S., & Aydos, M. (2019). Local image descriptor based Phishing web page recognition as an open-set problem. *European Journal of Science and Technology*, October, 444–451. https://doi.org/10.31590/ejosat.638404

Chatzichristofis, S. A., Arampatzis, A., & Boutalis, Y. S. (2010). Investigating the behavior of compact composite descriptors in early fusion, late fusion and distributed image retrieval. *Radioengineering, 19*(4), 725–733.

Chawla, N. V., Bowyer, K. W., Hall, L. O., & Kegelmeyer, W. P. (2002). SMOTE: Synthetic minority over-sampling technique. *Journal of Artificial Intelligence Research, 16*, 321–357. https://doi.org/10.1613/jair.953

Chen, K. T., Chen, J. Y., Huang, C. R., & Chen, C. S. (2009). Fighting phishing with discriminative keypoint features. *IEEE Internet Computing, 13*(3), 56–63. https://doi.org/10.1109/MIC.2009.59

Dalgic, F. C., Bozkir, A. S., & Aydos, M. (2018). Phish-IRIS: A new approach for vision based brand prediction of Phishing web pages via compact visual descriptors. *2018 2nd International Symposium on Multidisciplinary Studies and Innovative Technologies (ISMSIT)*, 1–8. https://doi.org/10.1109/ISMSIT.2018.8567299

Dunlop, M., Groat, S., & Shelly, D. (2010). GoldPhish: Using images for content-based phishing analysis. *5th International Conference on Internet Monitoring and Protection, ICIMP 2010*, 123–128. https://doi.org/10.1109/ICIMP.2010.24

Eroğlu, E., Bozkır, A. S., & Aydos, M. (2019). Brand recognition of Phishing web pages via global image descriptors. *European Journal of Science and Technology*, 436–443. https://doi.org/10.31590/ejosat.638397

Gao, H., & Chen, W. (2017). Image classification based on the fusion of complementary features. *Journal of Beijing Institute of Technology (English Edition), 26*(2), 197–205. https://doi.org/10.15918/j.jbit1004-0579.201726.0208

Google Safe Browsing | Google Developers. (n.d.). Retrieved January 30, 2021, from https://developers.google.com/safe-browsing

He, K., Zhang, X., Ren, S., & Sun, J. (2016). Deep residual learning for image recognition. *Proceedings of the IEEE Computer Society Conference on Computer Vision and Pattern Recognition, 2016-Decem*, 770–778. https://doi.org/10.1109/CVPR.2016.90

Huang, G., Liu, Z., Van Der Maaten, L., & Weinberger, K. Q. (2017). Densely connected convolutional networks. *Proceedings – 30th IEEE Conference on Computer Vision and Pattern Recognition, CVPR 2017, 2017-Janua*, 2261–2269. https://doi.org/10.1109/CVPR.2017.243

Jain, A. K., & Gupta, B. B. (2016). A novel approach to protect against phishing attacks at client side using auto-updated white-list. *Eurasip Journal on Information Security, 2016*(1). https://doi.org/10.1186/s13635-016-0034-3

Jain, A. K., & Gupta, B. B. (2017). Phishing detection: Analysis of visual similarity based approaches. *Security and Communication Networks, 2017*(i), 1–20. https://doi.org/10.1155/2017/5421046

Khandelwal, S., & Das, R. (2022). Phishing detection using computer vision. In S. Smys, R. Bestak, R. Palanisamy, & I. Kotuliak (Eds.), *Computer Networks and Inventive Communication Technologies* (pp. 113–130). Singapore: Springer.

Khonji, M., Iraqi, Y., & Jones, A. (2013). Phishing detection: A literature survey. *IEEE Communications Surveys and Tutorials, 15*(4), 2091–2121. https://doi.org/10.1109/SURV.2013.032213.00009

Li, B., Cheng, K., & Yu, Z. (2016). Histogram of oriented gradient based GIST feature for building recognition. *Computational Intelligence and Neuroscience, 2016*. https://doi.org/10.1155/2016/6749325

Lowe, D. G. (2004). Distinctive image features from scale-invariant keypoints. *International Journal of Computer Vision, 60*(2), 91–110. https://doi.org/10.1023/B:VISI.0000029664.99615.94

Nhat, H. T. M., & Hoang, V. T. (2019). Feature fusion by using LBP, HOG, GIST descriptors and Canonical Correlation Analysis for face recognition. *2019 26th International Conference on Telecommunications, ICT 2019*, 371–375. https://doi.org/10.1109/ICT.2019.8798816

Optical character recognition – Wikipedia. (n.d.). Retrieved January 30, 2021, from https://en.wikipedia.org/wiki/Optical_character_recognition

Phish-IRIS Dataset – A small scale multi-class phishing web page screenshots archive. (n.d.). Retrieved November 29, 2020, from https://web.cs.hacettepe.edu.tr/~selman/phish-iris-dataset/

Phishing definition & meaning | What is Phishing? (n.d.). Retrieved January 30, 2021, from https://www.webopedia.com/definitions/phishing-meaning/

Prakash, P., Kumar, M., Kompella, R. R., & Gupta, M. (2010). PhishNet: Predictive Blacklisting to detect Phishing attacks. *2010 Proceedings IEEE INFOCOM*, 1–5. https://doi.org/10.1109/INFCOM.2010.5462216

Rao, R. S., & Ali, S. T. (2015). A computer vision technique to detect Phishing attacks. *2015 Fifth International Conference on Communication Systems and Network Technologies*, 596–601. https://doi.org/10.1109/CSNT.2015.68

Rayar, F. (2017). *ImageNet MPEG-7 Visual Descriptors - Technical Report*, 21–23. http://arxiv.org/abs/1702.00187

Rosiello, A. P. E., Kirda, E., Kruegel, C., & Ferrandi, F. (2007). A layout-similarity-based approach for detecting phishing pages. *Proceedings of the 3rd International Conference on Security and Privacy in Communication Networks, SecureComm*, 454–463. https://doi.org/10.1109/SECCOM.2007.4550367

Szegedy, C., Liu, W., Jia, Y., Sermanet, P., Reed, S., Anguelov, D., Erhan, D., Vanhoucke, V., & Rabinovich, A. (2015). Going deeper with convolutions. *Proceedings of the IEEE Computer Society Conference on Computer Vision and Pattern Recognition*, 07–12-June, 1–9. https://doi.org/10.1109/CVPR.2015.7298594

Tola, E., Lepetit, V., & Fua, P. (2010). DAISY: An efficient dense descriptor applied to wide-baseline stereo. *IEEE Transactions on Pattern Analysis and Machine Intelligence*, *32*(5), 815–830. https://doi.org/10.1109/TPAMI.2009.77

Varshney, G., Misra, M., & Atrey, P. K. (2016). A survey and classification of web phishing detection schemes. *Security and Communication Networks*, *9*(18), 6266–6284. https://doi.org/10.1002/sec.1674

Wang, G. (2010). *Verilogo: Proactive phishing detection via logo recognition. January 2010*, 1–20. http://escholarship.org/uc/item/6m26d488.pdf

Wu, J., Cui, Z., Sheng, V. S., Zhao, P., Su, D., & Gong, S. (2013). A comparative study of SIFT and its variants. *Measurement Science Review*, *13*(3), 122–131. https://doi.org/10.2478/msr-2013-0021

Zero-day (Computing) – Wikipedia. (n.d.). Retrieved January 30, 2021, from https://en.wikipedia.org/wiki/Zero-day_(computing)

Index

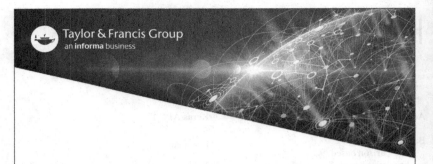

Printed in the United States
by Baker & Taylor Publisher Services